WORDSTAR® PROFESSIONAL MADE EASY

Walter A. Ettlin

Osborne **McGraw-Hill**
Berkeley, California

Osborne **McGraw-Hill**
2600 Tenth Street
Berkeley, California 94710
U.S.A.

For information on translations and book distributors outside of the
U.S.A., write to Osborne **McGraw-Hill** at the above address.

A complete list of trademarks appears on page 293.

WordStar® Professional Made Easy

1234567890 DODO 898

ISBN 0-07-881354-9

The manuscript for this book was prepared and submitted to Osborne/
McGraw-Hill in electronic form. The acquisitions editor for this project was
Jeff Pepper, the technical reviewer was Nick DiMuria, and the project editor
was Nancy Beckus.

Text body in Times Roman and display in Univers Bold. Cover art by Bay
Graphics Design Associates. Color separation by Colour Image. Cover sup-
plier, Phoenix Color Corp. Book printed and bound by R.R. Donnelly &
Sons Company, Crawfordsville, Indiana.

CONTENTS

ACKNOWLEDGMENTS

My sincere appreciation to my wife, Cynthia, and my secretary, Melody Martini, for their many hours of typing, testing instructions, and retyping the manuscript.

I am also grateful to Nick DiMuria, the technical editor, whose WordStar expertise did so much to catch my errors and omissions.

Thanks to the many contributors at Osborne/McGraw-Hill who gave that extra effort to hurry this manual through the various stages necessary to produce a book—Pamela Webster, design supervisor; Nancy Beckus, the project editor; Lindy Clinton, the associate editor; and Jeffrey Pepper, the acquisitions editor, who coordinated the efforts of all those involved.

—W.A.E.

INTRODUCTION

The purpose of this book is to help you become proficient with Word-Star. WordStar is a very flexible word processing program published by MicroPro International Corporation. This manual will give you the skills required for most types of general word processing assignments. The skills you acquire in completing the exercises in this book can be applied to word processors in any type of office.

Each lesson contains a set of instructions, sample exercises, and example text to be used in the lesson. If you have followed all the instructions, the text displayed on your screen or printed by your printer should match the example text in this book.

This book is not intended to replace the *WordStar User's Guide* published by MicroPro. The MicroPro manual supplements the command descriptions presented here and introduces other WordStar commands not covered in this book.

RELEASE 5

This latest update of WordStar, release 5, has several new features, including the ability to create newspaper-style columns and to open multiple files. The essence and feel of the original WordStar is available, but the standard opening screen now offers pull-down menus and the option of selecting commands with the arrow keys. The traditional commands and screens may be easily implemented by changing the Help level from 4 to 3. Files created by earlier releases can be used with WordStar 5 without modification.

Included as an integral part of WordStar is a dictionary that not only checks spelling, but contains definitions as well. Also in this release, WordFinder is automatically loaded each time you load WordStar.

WordStar comes with the three new supplementary programs: ProFinder, MailList, and TelMerge. Only ProFinder is discussed in this manual. ProFinder is for people who work with a hard disk. If you work with a lot of files —just WordStar files or files from a variety of programs—the sooner you become familiar with ProFinder, the easier your work will be.

A NOTE TO USERS OF EARLIER VERSIONS OF WORDSTAR

If you are an experienced WordStar user, you are familiar with much of the material in this book. To quickly take advantage of the new and modified material in WordStar 5, refer to Appendix A. It contains a list of this material along with a reference to the lesson where the material is discussed. In addition, throughout the book the symbol ⑤ in the margin points to the introduction of new material.

Even though you are probably very comfortable with the way you are currently using WordStar, try the new commands and the new screens. You may find some faster and easier ways to accomplish the word processsing tasks you perform daily.

INSTRUCTIONS FOR THE WORDSTAR COMMAND CARD

You will find the *WordStar Command Card,* located at the back of this book, a useful aid any time you are working with WordStar. The command card summarizes the most commonly used commands in the WordStar manual. You might want to remove it from this book and keep it near your computer for quick reference. The sooner you fully understand the commands listed on this card, the better you will be at using WordStar.

The symbol $^\wedge$ stands for the CONTROL (CTRL) key, which is located at the left side of the computer keyboard. The CTRL key is always used in conjunction with another key. Like a shift key, the CTRL key must be held down while the other key is pressed.

The code sent by the CTRL key does not register on the screen. It commands WordStar to perform some editing or formatting function, such as setting margins, underlining, or saving a document on the disk. You will use the CTRL key a great deal when working with WordStar.

MODIFYING WORDSTAR

WordStar release 5 default values and screens are used in the illustrations throughout this manual. Experienced users may wish to modify these values at this time. New users will probably find it to their advantage to become familiar with WordStar before customizing it. Keeping the default values has the advantage that your screens and printouts will match the illustrations in this book as you proceed. Examples and a discussion of how to modify WordStar are presented in Appendix C.

GETTING STARTED

When you are working with WordStar you are actually working with several computer programs: those that make up WordStar and those that make up your disk operating system, or DOS. (See Appendix B for more information about DOS.)

COMPUTERS

The only assumption this book makes is that you are working with a computer that will run WordStar 5. It makes no difference whether you are using a two-drive floppy system or a hard disk system, except if you are using a floppy system, you can ignore any discussion or reference to subdirectories. Appendix D offers a brief discussion about organizing your hard disk with subdirectories, along with some other DOS topics that are useful when working with WordStar.

This book also assumes that you have used WINSTALL to install WordStar on your hardware.

PRINTERS

The way you work with WordStar 5 varies little from one computer to another but the way printers work with WordStar is another matter. There is a wide variety of printers to attach to any PC. One of the major improvements of WordStar 5 over earlier versions is its ability to take advantage of the latest printer enhancements, such as selecting from a variety of fonts and font sizes, and printing a complete range of the graphics characters included with many of the newer printers.

Screen displays and sample printouts in this manual were produced on a printer that prints the extended IBM character and graphics set. The printer also has the ability to print up to double height and triple width if it is supplied with the appropriate Epson code. These are common printer characteristics and yours may have the same ability although it may use a different set of codes. At any rate, you will probably find it worthwhile to read your printer manual so that you can use WordStar to take advantage of its full range of printing abilities.

BACKGROUND FOR WORDSTAR

Before we get into the details of entering and editing a document in WordStar, let's go through some of the terminology and characteristics that are common to WordStar programs.

Default Values

Default values are values that WordStar automatically uses unless you change them. In the case of spacing, the default value is 1, or single spacing. Any default value may be changed with the appropriate command to suit the requirements of the document you are working with.

When you type a letter you, consciously or unconsciously, make many decisions about margins and other aspects of your letter that affect its appearance. WordStar supplies values for margins, tabs, and other layout characteristics of your work. The values supplied by

WordStar for these or any other functions are examples of default values. You can accept these values or change them to suit your needs. Each of these values will be discussed with the appropriate topic as you proceed through this manual.

WordStar's Commands

Two general categories of WordStar commands are used when you enter text in a file, Edit commands and Dot commands. The following lists show the common characteristics for each type of command.

EDIT COMMANDS The following are a few things you should know about Edit commands.

- The CTRL key, usually represented by the symbol $^\wedge$ in this manual, is pressed and held down while one or two other keys are pressed.

- An Edit command begins as soon as the command is given (ENTER is not pressed).

- Many of the more commonly used Edit commands can be executed by using the keypad arrows or function keys, or they can be selected from the pull-down menus.

The Edit commands fall into one of four general categories.

Command	Result
$^\wedge$O	Onscreen
$^\wedge$Q	Quick
$^\wedge$K	Block and save
$^\wedge$P	Print

DOT COMMANDS Dot commands perform a variety of functions but generally are related to printing and formatting a document. All dot commands begin with a period (hence the name, *dot command*) and are followed by two letters. The rules for placing dot commands are as follows:

- The period must always be placed in column one.

- The two letters may be upper- or lowercase.

- Only text that is part of the dot command is placed on the line with the command.

WINDOWS/MENUS/DIALOG BOXES

WordStar 5 uses windows, menus, and dialog boxes to communicate with the user. *Windows* is a general term that includes both menus and dialog boxes. A menu is a specific type of window that allows the user to make a selection. A dialog box is a window that provides information to the user and allows the user to supply requested information to WordStar. At times, both functions may occur in the same window.

In some cases, commands you select from a menu act immediately. For example, if you press **X** while in the File menu, you transfer immediately to DOS. For most commands, though, selecting a menu command produces a dialog box that may present you with some information but will always require at least one item of information before the command can be carried out. A suggested response may be displayed for you to accept or replace or you may have to type in a response. The dialog box may be as simple as the "DOCUMENT" box that is presented when you select D from the File menu.

Here only one item of information, the name of the file you wish to open, is requested.

Other dialog boxes may display the default values for several items.

You can edit any of these items or you can accept the default values as they are presented.

Dialog boxes have these common characteristics:

- All of WordStar's editing commands may be used to enter or edit information just as if you were editing a file.

- You may use the keypad arrow keys to highlight file names in a disk directory and then press ENTER to select the file.

- Press TAB or ENTER to move the cursor to the next field.

- Press SHIFT and TAB to move the cursor to the previous field.

- Press F10 to accept the displayed entries in the fields and to carry out the command.

- Press ESC or ^U to interrupt the command and return to the opening screen or the file being edited.

- Pressing ^R places in the field where the cursor is, the default values or the data displayed above or alongside the field.

The same dialog boxes display and, of course, operate the same whether they are arrived at by selecting commands from the traditional menus or from the new pull-down menus.

SELECTING COMMANDS

WordStar 5 offers two primary sets of command menus.

1. Traditional menus are the same style of menus found in earlier versions of WordStar.

2. Pull-down menus organize the commands differently but the commands themselves are still the same.

The option you work with is, of course, up to you. Throughout this book the instruction most commonly used will be to "select" a command. For example, select $^\wedge$KB to mark the beginning of a block. It's up to you whether you use the keyboard to enter $^\wedge$KB; use a function key, SHIFT-F9; open the Edit menu and use the arrow keys to select $^\wedge$KB; or use a mouse to select $^\wedge$KB.

HELP LEVELS

The screens that display when WordStar is loaded are those of help level 4, the level that offers selections from the new pull-down menus and dialog boxes. Of course, you may elect to change the help level to 3 or less to have your screen conform to the traditional WordStar help menus.

   The screens presented throughout this manual are those produced when commands are selected from help level 4, the new pull-down menus.

MAJOR CHANGES

WordStar 5 has some major additions including automatic hyphenation, windows to open two files, a variety of preformatted MailMerge forms, and the ability to work with multiple columns, to name just a few. Of prime consideration to users of earlier versions of WordStar is that all the old files are still usable and all the commands work very much as they have in the past. (See Appendix A for commands that have been modified.)

   New users will find that WordStar 5 is quicker and easier to learn and use with its windows and dialog boxes.

LOADING WORDSTAR

If your computer system is ready and you are logged onto the appropriate drive, type **WS**. (Characters you are to type are indicated in this book in boldface type.) After a brief copyright message the screen displays

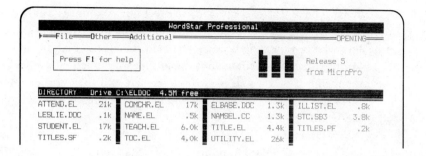

This opening menu provides three pull-down menus—**F**ile, **O**ther, and **A**dditional. To make a selection, you can use the left- and right-arrow keys or press one of the highlighted letters—F, O, or A. Pressing ENTER also selects the File menu, the most common selection. Even though the screen display shows uppercase letters, you can select a menu by typing the appropriate letter as upper- or lowercase.

FILE MENU

Press **F** (or ENTER) to open the File menu. The screen displays

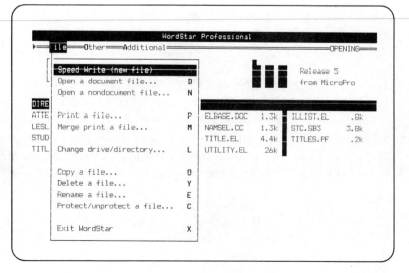

When you select a command, it executes as soon as you press the letter—either by performing its function or by displaying the dialog box where you enter the necessary additional information. In the following discussions, commands are grouped by function, as they are on the menu. If you would like to see the screen display for a command, press the desired letter and the dialog box is presented. To return to the menu press the ESC key.

One command, X, has no intermediate menu. Press **X** and you exit immediately to DOS; to return to WordStar you must reenter **WS** and press ENTER.

Opening a File (S, D, N)

S   Speed write (new file). Selecting S opens a file immediately and allows you to begin entering text. You enter the name for the file when you select one of the save commands.

D   Open a document file. Select D when you wish to edit a file you previously entered. You can also select D to open a new file. In this case you are required to enter a file name before you can begin entering text. You will press D for document file but not yet—wait until you are ready to start Lesson 1.

N   Open a nondocument file. The N option, for nondocument file, is used when you want to create a data file for merge printing or when you wish to write or edit a program using BASIC or another computer language.

Change Logged Drive/Directory (L)

Pressing L allows you to change the logged drive or subdirectory. Remember to use subdirectories to indicate the path. See Appendix D if the terms *path* and *subdirectory* are new to you. You can enter only drive names you designated as valid when you installed WordStar.

Print/Merge Print Commands (P, M)

Let's wait until appropriate files are available before discussing these topics. Printing is introduced in Lesson 3 and merge printing is covered in Lessons 17-19.

File Commands (O, Y, E, C)

The file commands require a text file in order to perform their functions. Because you are just starting and do not have a file to work with, we will not illustrate these now. These commands are presented in Lesson 3.

Return to DOS (X)

X   Exit WordStar. Pressing X returns you to DOS. Note the difference between selecting X and selecting R—discussed in the next section.

THE OTHER MENU (I, T, R, JJ, ?, ESC)

Selecting O displays the Other menu, a miscellaneous set of options.

I   Index a document. Indexing is covered in Lesson 16.

T   Table of contents. This option is covered in Lesson 16.

R   Run a DOS command. Pressing R allows you to exit WordStar and run other commands or programs from DOS. When execution is through, you can press any key to return to WordStar.

JJ   Help. Selecting JJ allows you to set the Help level. The default Help level is 4, giving you access to the pull-down menus. That is also the Help level used for the screen displays in this book.

?   Selecting ? gives you some statistical information about the computer's memory. An example of the screen display is shown here.

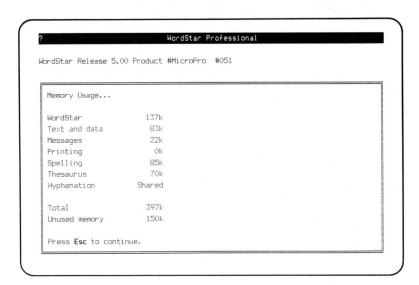

```
?                        WordStar Professional

WordStar Release 5.00 Product #MicroPro  #051


  Memory Usage...

  WordStar          137k
  Text and data      83k
  Messages           22k
  Printing            0k
  Spelling           85k
  Thesaurus          70k
  Hyphenation     Shared

  Total             397k
  Unused memory     150k

  Press Esc to continue.
```

ESC   Shorthand. Shorthand is a method of creating your own commands. You must select the ESC key by using an arrow key to highlight it—push the up-arrow once. Pressing the ESC key will perform its standard function of returning you to the previous menu. This topic is covered in Lesson 7.

ADDITIONAL MENU

Selecting **A** displays the Additional menu that gives you access to two supplementary programs provided with WordStar 5—MailList and TelMerge. These two programs are discussed in *WordStar Professional: The Complete Reference,* by Carole Boggs Mathews and Martin S. Mathews (Osborne/McGraw-Hill, Berkeley, Calif. 1988).

START A TEXT FILE

To begin word processing you'll use a *text* or *document* file. Whether you're entering text for the first time or correcting text, this process is referred to as *editing* a file.

To edit a file, first select **D** from the WordStar opening menu. You are presented with the DOCUMENT dialog box shown earlier. Type **EXAMPLE.1**. When naming a file, you may use up to eight letters or numbers, then a period, and a combination of up to three letters or numbers as an *extension* after the period (the extension is optional). Press ENTER. Your screen displays

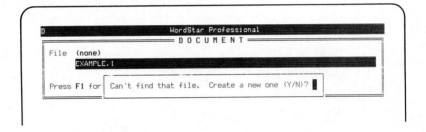

Because this is a new file, enter **Y**, and the screen immediately displays

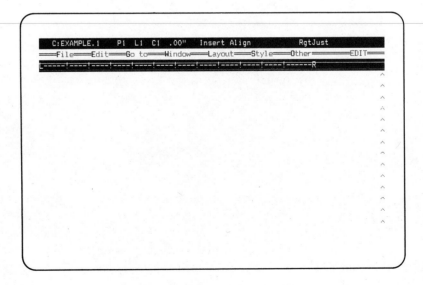

At the very top is the *status line* that tells you the drive you are logged into, the name of the file you are working on, the page number, the line number, and column number where the cursor is located. It also tells you that insert mode is on because the word "Insert" is displayed. Press the insert key (INS) at the lower right side of the keyboard. The message goes off. The INS key is a toggle. Press INS again to turn insert mode back on. Other information on the status line is discussed in appropriate lessons. The second line is the *menu selection bar* and the third line is the *ruler line*, which will be discussed at length in future lessons. Again, the screen displays used in this manual are with Help level 4 in effect.

A series of ^ symbols runs down the right side of the screen. The ^ symbol is one of a variety of *flag characters*. Flag characters always appear in column 80 of the screen. The significance of these flag characters will be discussed as appropriate throughout this book.

Now, on to Lesson 1.

CURSOR MOVEMENT SCROLLING

In the opening section, "Getting Started," you opened a file, or word processing document, named EXAMPLE.1. You will now enter some text into this file. Using the text in Example 1 at the end of this chapter, just start typing. Don't worry about typing errors now. Don't worry about pressing ENTER at the end of a line as you would do on a typewriter. As you type, press ENTER *only at the end of each paragraph.* Due to Word-Star's *word wrap* feature, which is on when you load WordStar, text that would extend past the right margin is automatically "wrapped around" to the left margin of the next line.

Watch the screen as you come to the end of a line and notice how the last letters of the last word on each line are aligned in the same column. This is called *right justification.* Text is right-justified by default. Extra spaces are inserted between words so that the last character of each line ends up at the right margin. To skip a line between paragraphs, simply press ENTER again. Don't worry about any mistakes; we'll take care of those in a later lesson.

Notice the *flag* character ($<$) in column 80. This symbol indicates that ENTER was pressed on that line. This flag character identifies, or flags, the end of any paragraph, the insertion of a blank line, or short lines of text, such as lines on a table of data.

CURSOR MOVEMENT (←, ↑, →, ↓)

The most common cursor movements are performed using the numeric keypad on the right of your keyboard. The movements most frequently used are performed with a single keystroke. For example, to move the cursor up, down, left, or right, press the arrow key that points in that direction; the cursor will move line by line or letter by letter. If you hold down one of the arrow keys, the cursor will move repeatedly in the direction indicated by the arrow. Notice what happens when the cursor is at the extreme right of a line and the right arrow is pressed once more: the cursor moves to the left end of the line below. When the cursor is on the last line of a paragraph and the down arrow is pressed, the cursor moves to the left side of the next line of the screen.

A note of caution: Loading WordStar automatically sets the numeric keypad to perform these cursor movements. If you should accidentally press the NUMLOCK (number lock) key, pressing the arrow keys will cause the number on each key to be inserted in the document. Should this happen, press NUMLOCK again to toggle the cursor movement function back into operation.

In addition to moving the cursor a single character or line at a time, you can move it directly to the top left corner of the screen by pressing the HOME key and to the bottom of the screen by pressing the END key. To move to the right or left end of a line, you use a combination of keys. Pressing ^QD (remember the symbol ^ represents the CTRL key and must be held down while you press the next letter) moves the cursor to the right end of a line, and pressing ^QS moves the cursor to the left end of the line. The following diagram illustrates this idea.

Top HOME

Left ^QS ◁   △
              ▽   ▷ ^QD Right

Bottom END

RIGHT WORD, LEFT WORD (^→, ^←)

Place the cursor at the left end of any line of text. Press ^→ four or five times and notice how the cursor moves quickly to the first letter of the word to the right. Now place the cursor at the right end of any line and press ^← several times. Notice how the cursor moves to the first letter of the word to the left.

MOVING FORWARD/BACKWARD
TO SPECIFIED CHARACTER (^QG, ^QH)

You can also move the cursor forward or backward to a specified character. To try this, move the cursor to the beginning of the first word of the second paragraph. Again you need to press **Q** while holding down the CTRL (^) key. To move forward, next press **G** (uppercase or lowercase). The top few lines on the screen clear, and a window with the question "Go to what character" appears. Enter a lowercase **w**. The cursor immediately moves over four words and rests at the first letter of the word *will*. Here, of course, it does make a difference if the letter you ask WordStar to find is uppercase or lowercase. If you had asked WordStar to find *W*, the entire paragraph would have been searched. The cursor would have come to rest at the end of the paragraph, and the message below would have been displayed in the window.

Could not find the file: W
Press ESC to continue

Following the same procedure, you can use ^QH to move backward to a specified character. Note that if you quickly enter a character after you press ^QB or ^QH, the cursor movement will occur without the question prompt being displayed.

MOVING TO END OF SENTENCE,
BEGINNING/END OF PARAGRAPH

In addition to moving to letters, you can move to punctuation marks, numbers, or any other characters displayed on the screen. For example, entering ^QG and a period in response to the question prompt moves the cursor directly to the next period. Usually the next period is at the end of the sentence in which the cursor rests, but it may come earlier or later, depending on how the sentence is punctuated. Pressing ENTER in response to the question prompt causes the cursor to move to the end of the paragraph if ^QG was pressed, or to the line above the beginning of the paragraph if ^QH was pressed. Note that if you ask WordStar to find the same character that the cursor is on, the cursor will not move in response to ^QG (forward search), but it will move in response to ^QH (backward search).

In addition to moving the cursor the short distances just discussed, you can also move it quickly to the beginning, end, or any given page of a file. These commands are discussed in later lessons which provide longer documents to work with.

SCROLLING (^PgDn, PgUp, ^PgUp, PgDn)

Scrolling may be a new term to you, so we will define it before we continue. Think of the text you entered into the computer as being on one long sheet of paper — a scroll. And think of the screen as an opening or window through which you can see only a small section of that one sheet of paper. When the window moves up that long sheet of paper and you see the material you have first written, you are scrolling *up,* and when the window moves down the sheet toward the end of the text, you are scrolling *down.*

The scrolling commands are very useful when you are reading a document on the screen. There are four of these commands: ^PgDn (scroll down line), PgDn (scroll down screen), PgUp (scroll up screen), and ^PgUp (scroll up line). To many people the references to up and down seem backward, but if you think of the screen as a window moving up or down over the material you have typed, then these terms make sense.

ENDING LESSON 1

When you have finished working with Example 1, save the file by pressing F10. The material you have just typed will be saved on the disk in the logged drive or on the logged subdirectory of the hard disk, and you will return to the opening screen. Select X from the File window to return to

DOS. (Saving documents will be discussed further in Lesson 3.) When you use this example text in Lesson 2, you'll be able to read it into the computer from the disk without retyping it. That's one of the advantages of word processing.

EXERCISES

1. Using Example 1, practice scrolling and moving the cursor to a predetermined position with as few keystrokes as possible.

Example 1

Most applications of microprocessing in our schools have been on a very small scale and, it seems to me, what we need at the moment is demonstration of specific benefits that might be realized from the purchase and installation of microcomputers. We currently have thirteen Apple II Plus computers at our school, but our program is an exception to the norm in public secondary education.

Our conference, therefore, will focus on the use of microcomputers in the public secondary school setting and will incorporate presentations designed to increase awareness in our administration of the potential benefits of having microcomputers in the schools. I envision presentations discussing the use of computers in the science curriculum, as multidiscipline tools, and for administrative applications.

MARGINS
HYPHENS
PARAGRAPHS
SPACING

In Lesson 1 you entered EXAMPLE.1. In this lesson you will enter a new example, but you will also edit EXAMPLE.1. Editing is probably the single most useful function of word processing. The full range of WordStar's edit functions will be introduced in this and the next few lessons. In Lesson 2 we will concentrate on changing the margins, hyphenation, reforming paragraphs, and changing the line spacing.

Load WordStar and when the opening screen appears, press ENTER or **F** to open the File menu. Select **L** to change your logged disk drive or subdirectory, if necessary, to the directory that contains EXAMPLE.1 and, after the selection is made and the opening screen of WordStar reappears, select **D** to open a document. You follow this procedure when you've already entered and saved a document and then want to edit it.

As soon as you select D, a new window appears with a prompt asking the name of the file you wish to edit. You want to edit the file you entered in Lesson 1. Select EXAMPLE.1 and press ENTER. Now appearing on the screen is the material you previously typed, including any mistakes you may have made.

The line above the text you entered is called the *ruler line*. Notice that the left and right margins of the material you typed correspond with the left and right ends of the ruler line. You change margins by adjusting the length of the ruler line. Other features of the ruler line will be discussed in Lessons 4 and 5.

WordStar offers two methods of setting the left and right margins. One method is to enter dot commands directly into the file. The other method is to use the commands ^OL or ^OR to display the MARGINS & TABS dialog box shown below.

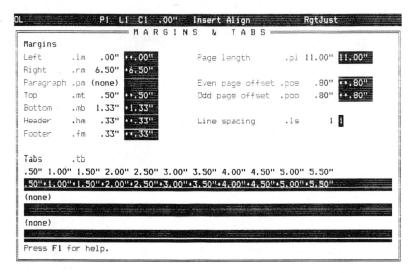

THE MARGINS AND TABS DIALOG BOX

A variety of dot commands is presented in this window, but for now we are only interested in two of them—the left and right margin commands. Before we proceed with the specifics of changing the left and right margins, let's consider the general characteristics of working with this dialog box.

- All entries are in decimal fractions of an inch (for example, .80 equals 8/10 or 4/5 of an inch).

(*Note:* Generally distances from the left or right side of the paper are measured to the nearest tenth of an inch since, most commonly, each screen column represents 1/10 of an inch. Those values pertaining to distances from the top or bottom of the paper are generally to the nearest hundredth of an inch. They normally represent multiples of 1/6 of an inch since, generally, lines on paper are printed 6 lines to the inch. Therefore, .33 represents 1/3 of an inch or two lines of text.)

- The values initially displayed are the default values supplied with WordStar.

- Any changes you make to the default values in this window will display in your file as dot commands when you return to the file. (You'll see an example of this shortly.)

- Pressing the space bar blanks the field the cursor is in.

- If a value is deleted in error, it may be reentered in the reverse video box by pressing $^\wedge$**R**.

- To enter a new value just type it in.

- Pressing the ENTER or TAB key moves the cursor to the next entry.

- To move the cursor backward press SHIFT-TAB; the cursor moves to its previous position in the window.

- When you return to the file, after changing a left or right margin value in this window, the dot command will display on a line *inserted above the first blank line preceding the cursor* (if the cursor is in the middle of a paragraph the dot command may display several lines above the cursor).

- Press F10 to accept changes made in the dialog box and return to the file.

- Press ESC to cancel changes made in the dialog box and return to the file.

You may enter as many changes to the left and right margins of a file as you like. The values that are in effect and display in the MARGINS & TABS dialog box are the ones that affect the file at the position of the cursor.

We will look at the specifics of the other commands in this window as each is introduced.

SETTING LEFT/RIGHT MARGINS

As mentioned previously, there are two methods of changing the margins. Let's start by using the MARGINS & TABS dialog box.

Changing the Margins Using
the Edit Commands (^OL, ^OR)

Press ^OL or press ALT-L and select Margins & Tabs from the Layout menu. When the Margins & Tabs window is displayed, the cursor will be opposite the command you entered to call it up. In this case it is shown opposite the left margin command (.lm). The command .LM (remember you can use either upper- or lowercase letters) is the dot command equivalent of the edit command ^OL.

As an example, change the left margin setting to .5 and press ENTER. Enter 5.00 for the right margin. Press F10 to return to the file and you will notice three changes. Refer to the illustration following the list of changes.

1. The L and R in the ruler line, representing the left and right end of the ruler line, have shifted.

2. At the top of the screen are the two dot commands, .LM .50" and .RM 5.00" indicating the changes you made in the Margins & Tabs window.

3. In the flag column, the flag is a dot. Dot commands will cause symbols to appear in the flag column, though these will not always be dots. (A complete list of the flag column characters is shown in Appendix B.)

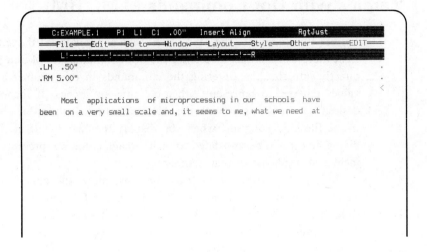

Move the cursor to the first text line of this file—in column one of the line containing "Most..." and press ENTER to move the text of EXAMPLE.1 down and produce a blank line. Move the cursor up with the arrow keys so it is in column 1 of the blank line. Type your name. As soon as you press the first letter it appears on the screen under the left edge of the ruler line. If you move the cursor back to the first letter of your name, you'll notice in the ruler line the cursor is indicated as being in column 6. The left margin is .50", as you entered. Of course, if you continue to type, the text you enter now will wrap at column 50 instead of column 65 as it did when you entered EXAMPLE.1.

To return the left and right margins to their default values, move the cursor to column one of the line containing .LM .50" and press the DEL key several times to delete the dot command. Do the same with .RM 5.00". If you return to the Margins & Tabs window, you will notice the default values of 0 and 6.5 inches have returned for the left and right margins, respectively.

Margins with Dot Commands (.LM, .RM)

Besides transferring to the Margins & Tabs window to set the left and right margins, you may also enter the dot commands, .LM and .RM, directly into the file. Entering the commands in this manner allows values entered to represent either columns or inches. If inches are desired, follow the value with the inch symbol ("). If the value entered in the file is in columns, when you display the MARGINS & TABS dialog box it will be translated to inches (each column represents 1/10 inch) and displayed in that manner.

To try this method of setting margins, move the cursor to the beginning of the second paragraph of EXAMPLE.1 and press ENTER to insert a blank line. Enter **.LM 3** and press ENTER. Now enter **.RM 70** and press ENTER (be sure the dots are in column one). Now let's consider what has happened.

First, notice the L and R in the ruler line have shifted to column 3 and column 70 respectively. Move the cursor above the .LM 3 and you'll see the default margins return. When the cursor again moves below the dot commands the new values will be reinstated.

Let's try another little experiment. Move the cursor after the 3 on the .LM 3 line and enter the inch symbol ("). Notice how the left margin indicator in the ruler line moves when you enter or delete this symbol. Try it. It changes the left margin from column 3, 3/10 of an inch, to column 30, 3 inches, depending on whether or not the inch symbol (") is there.

One more point to be aware of: lines containing dot commands do not affect line count since they do not print. They appear on the screen simply so you can be aware of the command. To see this, watch the line count in the status line as you move the cursor past the dot commands.

Relative Margins

In addition to setting specific left and right margins, in either columns or inches, you can also set left and right margins relative to existing margins. For example, in the previous section a left margin was set at column 3 and a right margin was set at column 70. If, at some later point in the file, you entered the command .LM + 7, the left margin would then be 10 (3 + 7). You can change the margins in this manner as often as you like. You can either increase the margin by entering a + value, or decrease it by using a − value. The change is always relative to the current margin. Again, the values may be in columns or inches and they also may be mixed. The same rules stated here for the left margin also apply to the right margin. The advantage is that if you change the initial specific left or right margin, then all subsequent relative margins (prior to any specific margins) also change automatically.

AUTOMATIC HYPHENATION
ON/OFF (^OH)

Sometimes it is desirable to hyphenate long words at the end of a line, particularly when you use a short ruler line of, for example, 50 columns or less. With WordStar 5, automatic hyphenation is on when you open a document file. The command to turn it off (or on—it's a toggle) is ^OH. With automatic hyphenation on, when you enter data or reformat a paragraph, hyphens will be inserted in words too long to fit at the end of the line.

"SOFT" HYPHENS (^OE)

If you wish, you can specify where hyphens will be placed with the command ^OE. To try this, position the cursor in a word where hyphenation can occur. Press ^**OE**. An equal sign appears at the position of the cursor to show you where the hyphen will occur should paragraph reformatting (discussed next) place the word where hyphenation might be helpful. The equal signs do not print when you print the file. If paragraph reformatting places the word in a position to be split, the equal sign will be displayed as a hyphen on the screen and when the document is printed.

REFORMING PARAGRAPHS (^B)

To make the effect of reforming paragraphs readily apparent on the screen, it is necessary to change the left, right, or both margins on the ruler line. I suggest that the minimum length of the ruler line be no less than 25 columns and the right end of the ruler line (the value following .rm in the Margins & Tabs window) be a number less than 80. We will discuss ruler lines that are longer than the screen width in a later lesson.

Before you try this command, turn automatic hyphenation off (^OH). Now using the dot commands, .LM and .RM, set the ruler line to a length different from that of the screen text.

Move the cursor to the first letter on the first line of the text in EXAMPLE.1. Press ^B. This adjusts, or *reforms,* all of the text in the first paragraph to fit within the margins determined by the new ruler line.

The cursor is now at the blank line between paragraphs. Press ^B twice to reformat the next paragraph as well. This process can be repeated to reformat all the material in any document, regardless of length.

Go back to the beginning of the first paragraph. Press ^OH again to toggle automatic hyphenation back on. Change the length of the ruler line. Reform the paragraph again by pressing ^B. It will depend on the margins you set but, most likely, at least one word was hyphenated. Experiment with these commands a bit to feel confident that WordStar will always hyphenate a word correctly. Also, try the "soft" hyphen command, ^OE, and change the margins to feel at ease with this command.

Pressing ^B starts the paragraph reformatting from the line where the cursor is currently positioned and will reform text until WordStar reaches an ENTER flag ($<$) (usually at the end of a paragraph). If you find that you have an unwanted ENTER flag in the middle of what should be a paragraph, here is one way to delete it. Use $^\wedge$**QD** to place the cursor at the end of the line with the ENTER flag. Press the DEL key (DEL is discussed in Lesson 4) until the line below jumps up to the end of the current line. Then press $^\wedge$**B** to reform the paragraph.

REFORMING AN ENTIRE DOCUMENT ($^\wedge$QU)

The process just described requires you to reform each paragraph individually. The command $^\wedge$**QU** allows you to reform multiple paragraphs, even an entire document with one edit command. Try this by changing the length of the ruler line, moving the cursor to the beginning of the file, and select $^\wedge$**QU** (Layout menu). Both paragraphs are quickly reformed. This command is most useful with long documents. Reformatting an entire document is discussed in detail in Lesson 5.

LINE SPACING ($^\wedge$OS)

With WordStar you can set the spacing of the material you type to anything from single spacing, as in Example 1, to one line of text every nine lines. You can also easily change the spacing of material that is already entered in a file. Let's try this now. Select $^\wedge$**OS**. Again you are presented with the Margins & Tabs window. The cursor is after the .ls (for line spacing) command, waiting for your entry. To double space, type **2**. Press the F10 key to return to the file. There are two screen indicators to show line spacing: in the status line you have the message "LinSp-2" and above the cursor is the dot command .LS2. Both are shown in the next illustration.

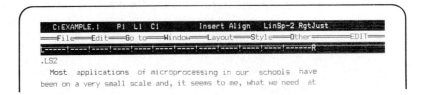

```
 C:EXAMPLE.1    P1  L1  C1          Insert Align   LinSp-2 RgtJust
====File====Edit====Go to====Window====Layout====Style====Other====EDIT====
L----!----!----!----!----!----!----!----!----!----!----R
.LS2
  Most  applications  of microprocessing in our  schools  have
been on a very small scale and, it seems to me, what we need  at
```

Now move the cursor to the beginning of the first paragraph and press ^**B** to reform the paragraph. You can repeat the ^B command to double-space both paragraphs, or you can use ^QU to automatically reform both paragraphs in sequence.

LINE SPACING BY DOT COMMAND (.LS)

You can also set line spacing with the dot command .LS. With the cursor in column 1, enter **.LS**. Follow the .LS with a value from 1 to 9 to set the desired line spacing. Using either the Margins & Tabs window or the dot command, you can have as many line space settings in your file as you like. Regardless of how they are set, the line space settings are saved with your file and are in effect the next time it is opened.

Using dot commands, set the spacing of your document to different values for each paragraph of Example 1. Type ^**QU** to reform both paragraphs to conform with the new spacing.

EXERCISES

1. Enter Example 2. Set the left margin to 5 and the right to 40. Reform the paragraphs to fit the margins.

2. Set the left margin to 1 and the right margin to 78. Reform the paragraphs to fit the margins.

3. In the Margins & Tabs window, set both the margins and the line spacing to new values for the first paragraph. Set different values for margins and line spacing for the second paragraph. Reform both paragraphs at the same time.

4. What would happen if you entered a number for the left margin that was larger than the number you entered for the right margin? Try it.

SAVING PRINTING OTHER FILE COMMANDS

All of the material that is placed on the disk is referred to as a *file*, whether it is something you type into the computer and save or a complicated commercial program like WordStar. WordStar has five commands to save a file plus one that abandons the file you are working with. First let's see why you might want to abandon a file and then why it's useful to have five ways to save a file.

ABANDON FILE(^KQ)

Suppose for some reason that after editing a file you decide the changes are not acceptable, and you would rather have your original version of the file than the corrections you just made. Select ^**KQ**; the following dialog box displays

```
Changes have been made.  Abandon anyway (Y/N)? █
```

Pressing Y will abandon the file without saving and return you to WordStar's opening screen. (The original version is still saved on the disk.) Pressing N will return you to where you were in the file.

This command is also useful if you are just experimenting with a new concept and you need a file to work with. For example, you may be learning WordStar 5 though you have considerable experience with an earlier version of WordStar. You can work with an existing file to practice new ideas and abandon the file when you are done to return it to its original condition.

SAVING FILES

Before we look at the individual save commands, note these general comments.

1. If you are editing a file that has been assigned a name, saving proceeds immediately when a save command is selected.

2. If you open a file using Speed Write, when you save the file, you will be presented with the SAVE AS dialog box shown below.

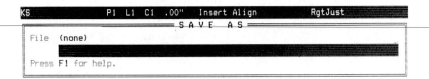

```
KS                    P1 L1 C1  .00"  Insert Align          RgtJust
                              S A V E   A S
File  (none)


Press F1 for help.
```

Use the standard naming procedures (maximum of eight letters for the name and three letters for the extension) to name the file.

3. If you previously edited a file during the current edit session, the SAVE AS dialog box will display the name of that file as the default file name.

Now let's look at the save commands.

Save and Reedit ($^\wedge$KS)

Using this command saves the material you have entered to the disk and then returns you to your document file so that you may continue editing. When you are working on a particularly long piece of material, you should save what you have typed about every 20 or 25 minutes so that you will not lose completed work if a power failure or other mishap occurs.

Save and Name ($^\wedge$KT)

You will probably find it useful at times to write a letter or other document based on an existing document. Using $^\wedge$KT you can save an existing document with a new name. Your original will be unchanged and have its same name. Selecting $^\wedge$KT presents you with the SAVE AS dialog box shown below.

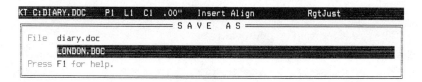

In the illustration above, I have entered LONDON.DOC in the File field as the name of the file where the edited version of DIARY.DOC will be saved. The document as originally stored on the disk in the file DIARY.DOC will remain unchanged.

Save and Exit File ($^\wedge$KD)

When you finish a document and want to continue using WordStar with a new file to edit, use $^\wedge$KD. It will save your file and return you to WordStar's opening screen.

Save and Exit (^KX)

This command saves the file you are working on and exits Wordstar, returning you to DOS or whatever exit destination you may have installed.

The fifth method of saving saves in conjunction with printing and is discussed in the following section.

PRINTING (P, ^KP, ^PRTSCR)

You can begin printing a document in three ways.

Print From File Menu (P)

If you have just entered WordStar or have saved a file and returned to the opening screen, you can select P (print) from the File menu. WordStar will present you with the PRINT dialog box similar to the one displayed below. (Note that if you previously edited a file, its name will be in the name field.)

Although this dialog box has a place for several entries, your normal procedure will be to enter the file name in the first field and press ESC to accept the default values for the remaining fields. Of course, the default value for the printer will depend on your installation. At times you may wish to change one or more of the default values, so let's look at each of them now. The default values, if any, are shown here in parentheses.

PAGE NUMBERS (ALL)   List the pages you want printed. Separate page numbers by commas. Successive pages are separated with a hyphen, e.g., 1,4, 7-9 will print pages 1,4,7,8,9.

ALL/EVEN/ODD (ALL)   Enter the single letter A, E, or O to select all pages, even pages, or odd pages.

PRINTER NAME   The name of the printer you selected during the installation process is displayed in this field. When the cursor advances to this field, a list of the other print drivers available to you is displayed at the bottom of the screen (again, those displayed are determined during the installation process). An example is shown here.

DIRECTORY	(HPLJET)	Printers				
630WP	ASC256	ASCII	ATT470	AUTOLF	CI8510	CITMSP
DRAFT	FX80	FX85	GEM10X	HPLJET	HPLJET2	IBMGRAPH
IBMPRO	IBMPROXL	LX80	MX80	NEC8023	NX1000	P1090
P351SX	RX80	TYPEWR	XTRACT			

As usual, you may use the arrow keys to select and substitute one of the drivers for the default value.

PAUSE BETWEEN PAGES (N)   Press ENTER (for "no") when using continuous paper (the default selection). When using single sheets of paper, press **Y**; printing will pause to allow you to insert a new sheet of paper for each page.

USE FORM FEEDS (Y)   If you are using single sheets of paper, or if your printer does not have a top-of-form setting, you will not want to use form feeds. Enter **N**. Be sure to use dot commands to set paper length. If you are using continuous-form papers and your printer has a top-of-form setting, printing will be faster and more accurate if you enter Y (or press ENTER) to use the form-feed option (the default selection).

NONDOCUMENT (N)   You usually will press N or ENTER (the default selection). Nondocument mode is discussed in Lesson 17, which discusses merge printing.

NUMBER OF COPIES (1)   The default value is one copy. If you want more than one, just enter the number and press ENTER.

Finish Edit and Print (^PrtScr)

When you have finished editing a document, you can save that document to a disk and immediately begin to print it by pressing ^PrtScr. This again displays the PRINT dialog box. Answer the questions as described above. *Note:* If the file was opened using Speed Write, you are presented with the SAVE AS dialog box and returned to the opening screen after saving.

Print While Editing (^KP)

While editing one document, you can print a different document. To do this select ^KP. The small dialog box shown below is displayed.

```
Print or merge print (P/M)? ▌
```

Entering P for print presents the PRINT dialog box and the procedure is the same as that described above. Selecting M gives you the Merge Print option. The Merge Print option will be discussed in Lesson 19 after MailMerge is introduced.

Let us now use some of these options. Suppose you have just printed a four-page document and discovered something on page 3 that must be corrected. You return to WordStar, load your document, and make the necessary corrections. You save the document and prepare it for printing by pressing ^PrtScr. Press ENTER at the File field and at the Page Numbers field enter **3** and press ENTER. Press ESC to enter the default responses for the remaining questions.

You can interrupt printing that is in progress by selecting the letter P. Pressing P displays the following menu:

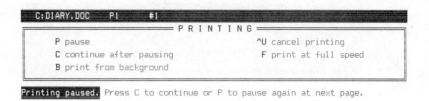

You can now select the response you wish by pressing the appropriate key (note that to cause the printer to pause, you must press P again). How quickly the printing stops after you select P or ^U depends on your printer. These selections stop the flow of data to the printer, but the data stored in the printer will continue to print until it is exhausted.

OTHER FILE COMMANDS FROM THE OPENING MENU

There are four other file commands that can be accessed from the opening File window: Copy (O), Delete (Y), Rename (E), and Protect (C). Select one of these commands and you are presented with a dialog box. You may then type in the file names or use the arrow keys to select the desired file.

Copy (O)

This option allows you to copy a file from one disk to another, one directory to another, or to copy a file onto the same disk under another name. Press **O** and the COPY dialog box shown here is displayed.

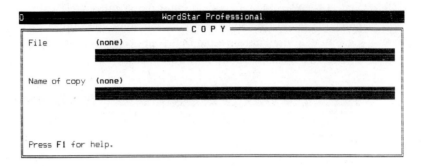

Select the file names for File and Name of copy and the copying takes place. If you enter a file name that already exists, a new window will open and it will inform you. You then press ESC to continue.

Delete (Y)

Press **Y** and this DELETE dialog box is displayed.

Use this option to delete any file in your disk. You will use this command frequently to rid your disk of files you no longer need.

Rename (E)

Use this option to change the name of a disk file. Press **E** and the screen displays a dialog box similar to the one used with Copy. Let's try this command, using the file EXAMPLE.1. In the Current name field enter **EXAMPLE.1**. In the New name field enter **EXAMPLE.X** and press ENTER.

Notice that the name on the directory has changed. You would now load your original EXAMPLE.1 text by entering the file name **EXAMPLE.X**. WordStar will not allow you to change a name to that of a file already on the directory. Using the same procedure, change the name back to the original, because we will refer to EXAMPLE.1 in later lessons.

Protect (C)

The protect option allows you to "lock" a file. You can then examine the file, but you cannot change it in any way. Using the protect option will also prevent other WordStar users from accidentally changing your file. Press **C** and a dialog box similar to that of Delete is presented.

Let's try this. From the File menu press **C**. In the File field enter **EXAMPLE.1** and press ENTER. A window opens telling you the status of the selected file and asking, in this case, to confirm that you want to protect it. Enter **Y**, the file is protected and you return to the Opening menu. If you open the file now, the status line will display "Prtect" to indicate a protected file.

With each of these file commands you may, of course, precede your file name with a disk drive option (for example, B:EXAMPLE.1) or subdirectory (for example, \WS5\EXAMPLE.1).

EXERCISES

1. Save the file you have in the computer and enter **EXAMPLE 3**. Name the file EXAMPLE.3. Type the entire example and then use the cursor controls to go back and correct any errors.

2. Use EXAMPLE.3 to practice changing spacing, scrolling, changing the ruler line, and reforming paragraphs.

3. Save EXAMPLE.3 and print it. (After editing a file, be sure to save it before you print it. The material printed is the last version of your file saved on the disk.)

Example 3

```
Memo to:      Bill Smith

From:         John Regal

Some of the computer projects we are now working on will require
work after the close of the school year this June and prior to
the opening of school in September.

The projects are

1.  Martinez  Elementary School class lists and state attendance
reports

2.   Las Juntas class lists and state attendance reports

3.   Attendance register for special education

With these and additional pending assignments in mind, I would
like to discuss with you compensation for myself and a clerical
assistant to handle this workload outside the regular school
year.


JR/ljp

May 31, 1989
```

TABS
CENTERING
DELETING
UNDELETING
INSERTING

You have already been introduced to the ruler line. When you begin editing a document, its left and right ends are set to WordStar's default values. These values are at column 1 for the left end and column 65 for the right end. Initial tab stops are also set. To work with the topics in this lesson, open a file with Speed Write. Now check the default tab values by displaying the MARGINS AND TAB dialog box on the screen or look back to Lesson 2 where it is illustrated.

TAB (TAB)

To advance the cursor to the next tab stop, press the TAB key. If insert is on, which it is by default, and text is to the right of the cursor, when you press TAB the text will move to the right the same number of spaces the cursor moves.

SETTING TABS (.TB)

Sometimes the default tab settings are not appropriate for the material being entered. You have a variety of ways of setting tab stops with WordStar. We'll examine two of them in this lesson. Let's start with the dot command .TB. With the cursor in column 1 enter **.TB**. Notice the tab stops normally shown in the ruler line are no longer there.

Enter 15, a space, and 40.

There are now exclamation marks on the ruler line at columns 15 and 40 to indicate tab stops. Between the numbers you enter on the dot command line for tab stops, either commas or spaces may be used as separators. A file may contain as many different tab dot commands as you like.

While you are editing and the cursor moves toward the end of the file, the last dot command the cursor passed is the one in effect. If the cursor is moving from the end of the file toward the beginning of the file, the tab command it is approaching is the one in effect. If there are no tab commands between the cursor and the beginning of the file, the ruler line displays the default tabs.

Note: For users of earlier versions of WordStar, ^ON is no longer used with tabs, so the command is now used to display the Notes (footnotes, endnotes) menu. This menu will be discussed in Lesson 15.

DECIMAL TABS (#)

The same procedure just used to set standard tab stops can also be used to set decimal tabs. Move the cursor after the 40 on the .TB command line, press the space bar, and type # (number sign) **60**. On the ruler line you now have a "#" at column 60.

```
              P1  L1  C1  .00"   Insert Align          RgtJust
    ═══File═══Edit═══Go to═══Window═══Layout═══Style═══Other═══════EDIT═══
    L═════════!═══════════════════════!═══════════════#═══R
     .tb 15 40 #60
```

To see how decimal tabs work, press ENTER so that the cursor is in the line below the tab dot command and press TAB three times. Notice that when the cursor moved to column 60, the message "Decimal" appeared in the status line. Now watch the screen and type the number **$1,240.49**. First type **$1,240**; as the number is typed, the cursor stays in the same position, and each character you enter forces the previously entered characters to move left. Now enter the decimal point. It takes the position of the cursor, which moves to the right. Notice also that the "Decimal" message no longer appears in the status line. As you type **49**, the numbers are entered at the right in the normal manner.

PARAGRAPH TAB (^OG)

A special tab is paragraph tab. It allows you to temporarily reset your left margin. Pressing ^OG once sets the left margin to the first tab on the ruler line. Each successive pressing of ^OG temporarily moves the left margin of the ruler line one additional tab stop to the right. The position of the temporary left margin is denoted visually on the ruler line by replacing the exclamation mark with the letter *V*. The illustration below shows the ruler line after ^OG has been pressed twice.

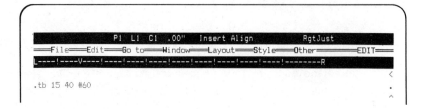

In this illustration, the cursor is above the dot command so the default tabs are displayed. (The procedure to insert a blank line is discussed further in this lesson.) The common use of paragraph tab is to reform indented questions or paragraphs. The ruler line automatically returns to the original left margin after you press ENTER or reform a paragraph.

EMBEDDING A RULER LINE (^OO)

After you have changed the tabs and/or margins on the ruler line, you may want to save the ruler with your document. That way, the next time you open the document for editing, the ruler line you created previously will be in affect starting at the point where it was embedded. To try this, place the cursor in column 1 of a blank line and enter **^OO**. A copy of the ruler line is duplicated in your document.

Ruler lines created in this manner will not print when the document is printed. The symbol '.RR' on the left is the dot command used to establish a new ruler line. The ruler line will function only if the dot is in column 1. This and other ruler line dot commands will be discussed extensively in Lesson 5. In preparation for the next section use Speed Write (select **S** from the File menu or Opening menu) to open a new file.

CENTERING (^OC)

Look at Example 4B. It requires centered text at the top of the page. To enter this heading move the cursor to column 1, line 1, and type **STRAND HIGH SCHOOL**. Now press ^OC, and the material you typed will be centered within the ruler line. Press ENTER to end the line and then enter the next three lines, using ^OC to center each line of text.

VERTICAL CENTERING (^OV)

In addition to using ^OC to center text on the ruler line you can also center text vertically using ^OV. Centering text vertically will only center text midway between the last line of the page and the last line that can have text on the page. For example, suppose the bottom line of the page is 36 and you enter text to be centered on that line. If the page has default top and bottom margins and you press ^OV to center the text, the text will move to line 45 of the page. The text will not change columns. You will need to use ^OC, either before or after centering vertically, to center the text horizontally (on the ruler line).

Note: Any blank lines —lines with the carriage return symbol ,<, in the flag column — below your text will also be centered.

CENTERING DOT COMMAND (.OC ON/OFF)

If the material you are centering involves more than one line (as the heading for this example does), you may find the dot command .OC a more convenient method to center. The command .OC ON turns centering on. Let's enter this heading again, this time using the centering dot command. To try this, enter the dot command ^.OC ON on the next line and press ENTER. Again enter the heading from Example 4B. This time the heading is automatically centered. When the section you want centered is complete, place the cursor in column 1 of the line following that section and enter .OC OFF.

Using the centering dot command also has the advantage of staying in effect anytime you return to the file for editing. Should some information in the heading change at a later time, just reenter it and it will automatically center.

DELETING (DEL, BACKSPACE, ^T, ^Y, ^QY, ^QDEL, ^QT)

When you enter or edit a document, you may make errors or want to revise your work. Frequently you will want to delete text. There are several ways to delete small amounts of text:

Command	Action
DEL	Deletes the character above the cursor.
BACKSPACE (←)	Deletes the character to the left of the cursor.
^T	Deletes an entire word at a time or the portion of the word to the right of the cursor (reads to the next punctuation mark or space).
^Y	Deletes an entire line and its space. The cursor may be any place in the line. The text below moves up to replace deleted text. Note difference with ^QY when the cursor is at the beginning of a line.
^QY	Deletes everything on the line from the position of the cursor to the right end of the line. If ^QY is entered at the beginning of a line, it deletes all text but leaves a blank line.
^QDEL	Deletes text on the line to the left of the cursor (similar to ^QY).
^QT	Deletes from the cursor to the designated character. ^QT. (period) deletes from the cursor to the end of a sentence. ^QT (ENTER) deletes from the cursor to the end of a paragraph.

Use the appropriate command from the list above to delete unwanted material from the current file so that you may use it later to complete Example 4B.

The next section discusses how to "undelete," or undo, a deletion. Try each of the preceding commands in conjunction with the Undo command.

UNDO (^U)

It can be very frustrating to press ^Y instead of ^T and delete a whole line of text when you intended to delete a single word. The Undo command restores deletions. Specifically, it restores the text deleted by the commands ^Y, ^T, ^KY, ^QDEL, ^QT, and ^QY. It does not restore single characters deleted using the DEL or BACKSPACE key. Those can be undone more easily with a single keystroke by reentering them.

You can restore text by pressing ^U, the undo command. The deleted text will be inserted starting at the position of the cursor.

You can also use Undo to move or copy a small portion of text. Use the appropriate delete command to delete the word, line, or paragraph you want to move. Move the cursor to the position where you want the text inserted and press ^U. To copy text, first *delete* the text to copy. Without moving the cursor, press ^U to restore it to its original position. Move the cursor to the new position and again press ^U. The text appears again. Text can be restored any number of times, so long as you do not issue another delete command. The text is stored by Word-Star until it is replaced by text deleted by another delete command. Procedures for moving or copying larger amounts of text are described in Lesson 8.

A word of caution. Accidentally pressing ^U will place the line of text in your file that you previously deleted. Keep in mind that ^U serves two functions: it undoes deletions and interrupts commands in progress. If a command you intend to interrupt has completed execution, pressing ^U will cause the Undo function to be performed.

INSERTING (INS)

You may have noticed the "Insert on" message on the status line. The INS key controls whether insert mode is on or off. If insert mode is on, you can press INS to turn it off; the message on the status line also will be turned off. Press the INS key again to turn insert mode on again. The Edit menu also shows that you can turn this function on and off by pressing ^V.

When insert mode is on, any character you type will be entered to the left of the cursor, and all text following the inserted character will be moved to the right. You can insert characters, tab spaces, and entire lines. To insert a blank line, place the cursor at the left margin of the line that should follow the blank line, and press ENTER.

To add words to a paragraph, you move the cursor to where you want the word to start and type it in. To illustrate, let's add a couple of words to our text from Example 1.

microprocessors and

```
            Most applications of microprocessing in our schools have
been on a very small scale and, it seems to me, what we need at
the moment is demonstration of specific benefits that might be
realized from the purchase and installation of microcomputers.
```

Move the cursor to the beginning of the word *microprocessing*, press INS (if the insert mode is not on) and then type **microprocessors and**. As you type, the paragraph is automatically reformatted.

EXERCISES

1. Open a file as EXAMPLE.4A. Set up a ruler line with tabs at 25 and 50 and with a right margin at 75. Enter the six names and addresses of Example 4A. Practice deleting with this file. Be sure you can quickly delete names in the left, right, and middle columns without disturbing those names you don't wish to delete.

2. Enter Example 4B if you have not already done so. Use delete, undelete, and insert to quickly correct any errors you may make.

3. You now have all the commands necessary for efficient editing of a document. Starting with Example 1, proofread and correct any errors in the examples you have previously entered and saved.

Example 4A

```
Veronica Lopez          Mark Jones              Lisa Maxwell
520 Ridgeville Drive    872 Olivet Road         956 Bristol Road
San Jose, CA  94395     Alma, IL  98432         Lyman, WA  59874

Mary Lewis              Sam Parker              Julie Rogers
120 Colgate Road        754 Alameda Drive       504 Sucrest Lane
Steele, MI  65753       Downey, ID  45634       Alto, TX  59735

Susie Waldo             Johnny O'Brien          Greg Saunders
2321 Brisbon Lane       483 Virginia Street     384 Sunset Road
Shook, MI  46843        Chula, GA  28723        Lott, TX  96746
```

Example 4B

```
                        STRAND HIGH SCHOOL
                          415 Green Street
                         Concord, CA  94520
                          (415) 798-5209


Mr. Ron Hubbard
Alhambra High School
211 C Street
Martinez, CA  94553

Dear Mr. Hubbard:

The high school data base is being tested at Martinez High
School.  Testing of the report generator for these programs will
begin this week as well, also at Martinez High School.

Any suggestions for additional information or functions to be
incorporated in the data base should be given now.  It is more
cost effective to incorporate changes now than to wait until the
project is complete.  All high school principals and their
secretaries and the high school nurses should review the programs
and make suggestions.

Any information that needs to be prepared for transfer to the
district office computers should be outlined by the appropriate
district administrator.

I am available to demonstrate the software at any time.  Please
have those reviewing the software return any suggestions,
comments, criticisms, etc., to me by December 19.

Sincerely,


Walt Elison
```

RULER LINE MARGIN RELEASE NEWSPAPER-STYLE COLUMNS

In Lesson 2 you changed the left and right margins of the ruler line by using the MARGINS & TABS dialog box and also by entering .LM and .RM directly into the file. In this lesson you'll learn additional ways to change margins and other features of the ruler line.

RULER LINE SYMBOLS

There are seven symbols that can appear on the ruler line. Six of them, L, R, − , ! , #, V, have already been discussed. The remaining one, P, is presented in this lesson. The table below shows all seven and what each represents.

Symbol	Represents
L	Left margin
R	Right margin
P	Paragraph margin
!	Tab column
#	Decimal tab column
V	Temporary indent
—	Columns between margins

RULER LINE (.RR)

Another method used to set the ruler line with appropriate margins and tabs is the dot command, .RR. To try this command using Speed Write, open a file and, with the cursor in line 1, enter **.RR**. Keep the cursor on the same line and enter dashes with tabs (exclamation marks) at columns 15, 30, and 45. Place the last dash in column 50 and press ENTER. Your screen should match the following illustration.

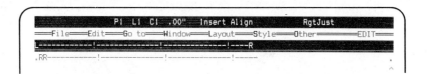

Note that the left margin is specified in the status line as column 1. If you want the left margin to be in column 10, you start the dashes in column 10.

When using this method to establish the ruler line, you must follow special procedures to place the left margin in column 2 or 3 (where the R's are). Let's try this now. With the cursor in column 1 enter **.RR**, press ^P, and press ENTER. Press the SPACEBAR to move the cursor to column 2.

Enter a few dashes to establish your ruler line and press ENTER. Enter a character to verify that it appears in column 2. Also note that another symbol, a minus sign, appears in the flag column. This flag means that the material on the indicated line and the next are continuous.

PARAGRAPH MARGIN (.PM)

Another dot command that's useful with the ruler line is the Paragraph Margin command, .PM. Just as with the left and right margin commands (.LM and .RM), this command may be entered through the MARGINS & TABS dialog box or directly into the file using .PM. Also just as with the margin commands, .PM values entered in the file may be in either columns or inches. Again, if you want the value in inches, follow it with the inch symbol (").

Placing this command in a file causes the first line following a carriage return to be indented the number of spaces you specify. For example, entering **.PM 7** will indent the first line of the paragraphs that follow by seven spaces. Also, note that entering .PM 7 causes a P to appear in the ruler line in column 7. The illustration below shows an example.

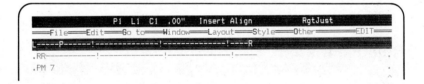

With the .PM command you can quickly place paragraph indentations in a file. Enter **.PM** followed by a space and the desired value at the top of the file and select $^\wedge$**QU**. All paragraphs will be reformed with the selected indentations. You can use this procedure with documents of any length and of course you can use .PM commands with different indentations throughout your document. Note that the .PM command will not eliminate indentations placed in the file with the TAB key.

Hanging Indent

Another useful application of the paragraph margin command is to use it for a "hanging indent." An example of this is entering a set of numbered questions as illustrated in Example 5 at the end of this lesson. The procedure is shown in the following illustration.

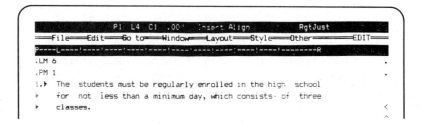

The dot command .LM 6 is used to set the left margin for the questions. Paragraph margin, .PM, is used to set the column where question numbers will print, in this case in column 1. Enter the number and a period, press TAB to move the cursor to the left margin at column 6. The question is entered now within the left and right margins. After ENTER is pressed at the end of question 1, you follow the same procedure to enter the number for the next question.

Relative Margin

Just as you set relative left or right margins in Lesson 2, you can also set a relative paragraph margin. For example, if you enter .PM +3 while a .PM 7 is in effect, your new paragraph margin would be 10. This has the advantage that changing the initial .PM command in the file changes all subsequent PM commands.

You have a variety of methods now to set margins, tabs, and indentations. Become familiar with all of them so that you can use the one best suited to a particular situation. Be sure to embed a nonprinting ruler line in sections of your file where the ruler line changes. This saves much time on subsequent edits.

PREFORMATTED RULER LINES

In addition to using the .RR command to create a ruler line, WordStar comes with four preformatted ruler lines, .RR 0 through .RR 3. To look at one of these, move to the end of the file and place the cursor in column 1. Enter **.RR 1**. (Since .RR 0 is the default ruler line, you wouldn't see any change.) You'll notice the ruler line changes as the 1 is entered. Generally it is worthwhile to place the ruler line in the file by moving the cursor below the dot command and entering $^\wedge$**OO**. This gives you the opportunity, during later edits, to see the ruler line before the cursor comes to the dot command. The following illustration shows the screen after using $^\wedge$OO.

You can have up to 10 preformatted ruler lines in WordStar (.RR 0 through .RR 9). To create your own ruler lines use WSCHANGE (see Appendix C). In addition to creating ruler lines 4 through 9 you can also use WSCHANGE to change the four, R0-R3, that are supplied.

PARAGRAPH REFORM
/WORD WRAP ON/OFF (.AW)

At times you will not want certain elements of your document, such as charts and graphs and so on, to be affected by paragraph reformatting. Bracket these sections with the dot command, .AW. The command .AW OFF turns off paragraph reformatting, and .AW ON turns it back on for the remainder of the document or until you enter another .AW OFF. Besides paragraph reformatting, this dot command also turns off word wrap and justification—which means you can have a portion of the document displayed and printed ragged right. Notice that when the cursor is in a section of the document where .AW OFF is in effect, "Align" no longer appears in the status line.

With the variety of commands you have available now to control margins and formatting, you will find it easy to use ^QU to reformat entire documents—even long and complex documents. The key is to place an appropriate ruler line preceding each section and to use .AW ON/OFF in sections where reformatting is not desired.

MARGIN RELEASE (^OX)

Another command available to allow data entry outside the ruler margins is ^OX, the margin release command. To try this, set your left margin to 10. With the cursor in column 1 press **^OX**. The message "Mar-Rel" for margin release appears in the status line. You can now enter information at the position of the cursor—outside the margins. Press **^OX** again to turn margin release off and the next character key you press will print at the left margin.

NEWSPAPER-STYLE COLUMNS (.CO, .CB, .CC)

WordStar now gives you the capability of working with newspaper-style columns. You can use the three dot commands in the following list.

.CO n,t	Defines the number of columns on each page (designated by n) and the spacing between columns (indicated by t). The space represented by t can be in either character columns or inches.
.CB	Sets a column break; it corresponds to .PA in a standard WordStar file.
.CC n	Sets a conditional column break. It places a pagebreak if there are not n

lines remaining on the page. It corresponds to .CP in a standard Word-Star file.

For example, to establish two newspaper-style columns with four-tenths of an inch (or four character columns) between them, use the dot command .CO 2, 4.

The width of the text columns is established in the usual manner with left and right margin commands. Columns of this type do not appear side by side on the screen but do appear side by side when printed. A sample screen display of columns follows.

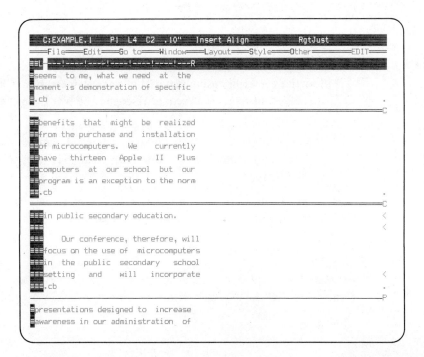

In this example, page breaks were set after six lines to display the screen enhancements that indicate newspaper-style column breaks. Using EXAMPLE.1, type **.CO 3, 4** to set the number of columns, and **.RM 35** to set the column width. The symbols, ≡, on the left of the screen tell you which of the three columns you are working with. Notice in the flag column a C is used to indicate the end of a column and, as usual, a P to designate the end of a page. These flags, C or P, occur if column/page ends happen by default or are forced by using .CB.

If you have a graphics monitor you can select Preview, ^PO, to view the page. Preview is discussed fully in Lesson 21. To return to standard column structure, enter .CO or .CO 1. You can also change any existing newspaper-style columns back to standard columns by deleting the dot commands associated with newspaper columns.

EXERCISES

1. Enter the letter in Example 5. It has sections requiring ruler lines of different lengths. Make up a model for each.

2. Practice centering, using material of your own creation. Change the length of the ruler line and re-center the words on the new ruler line.

3. Practice typing text outside the margins, using material of your own creation. Reform a paragraph that has text outside the left margin.

4. Experiment, using one of your existing files, with different numbers and widths of newspaper-style columns.

Example 5

```
                    STRAND HIGH SCHOOL
                     415 Green Street
                    Concord, CA  94520
                     (415) 798-5209

Dear Student Employer:

Please be advised that one of our students who has been employed
by you has applied for credit in the Outside Work Experience
Program.

We would like to acquaint you with the basic requirements of this
program so that there is no misunderstanding at a later date.

Requirements

1.   The student must be regularly enrolled in the high school
     for no less than a minimum day, which consists of three
     classes.

2.   Absence from school automatically is considered absence
     from the Outside Work Experience job station.  It is
     generally considered that if a student cannot attend
     school, he cannot go to work.

3.   A student cannot be employed in excess of eight hours per
     day, including school time.

     Example

     If a student has four classes in the morning, and works
     four hours after school, he is within the requirements.
     However, if a student has a full class schedule, he will
     be entitled to work four hours after school.

4.   All students under the age of eighteen must have a duly
     issued work permit.

I hope this letter is informative and that you and your employee
will be able to comply.  We would like to express our
appreciation for your cooperation.  If you have any questions,
please call me at 932-8976.

                         Yours very truly,



                         JOHN SMITH
```

SPECIAL PRINT FUNCTIONS

There is a wide variety of printers with varying capabilities on the market. WordStar can take advantage of the characteristics of most of them. The three primary categories of printers are daisy wheel or thimble, dot matrix, and laser. You will have to consult your printer manual to determine whether your printer can take advantage of the commands discussed in this lesson. Most of the newer printers can.

After you have opened a file, the special print functions are accessed through the Style menu or by pressing $^\wedge$**P** and selecting from the traditional WordStar menu. The two most commonly used special print functions are underlining, $^\wedge$PS, and boldfacing, $^\wedge$PB.

To get started with the print functions, open a file and enter Example 6A.

PRINT DISPLAY ON/OFF ($^\wedge$OD)

Before proceeding, note that the display of control characters on the screen can be toggled on and off. To turn the control character's display off, select $^\wedge$**OD**. The screen returns to normal, with only the feature itself (such as underlining or boldfacing) displayed. Selecting $^\wedge$**OD** again turns the display back on.

Note that when you print a file, these control character symbols do not print, even if they are toggled on to appear on the screen. In addition to eliminating the display of control characters, pressing $^\wedge$**OD** also eliminates the display of tabs and soft hyphens.

UNDERLINE ($^\wedge$PS)

You can underline a single letter or an entire document. All that is necessary is to bracket the text you want underlined with the appropriate code. In the document, we will underline the words *print functions*. Position the cursor on the *p* in *print* and, with insert on, select $^\wedge$**PS**. Everything from that point on is underlined. Position the cursor immediately after the *s* in *functions* and again select $^\wedge$**PS**. Now only *print functions* is underlined. Besides being underlined, *print functions* is also bracketed by the symbol $^\wedge$S.

When you print, the underlining will appear just like it does on the screen—only the words, not the spaces between words, are underlined. However, you can tell WordStar to use continuous underlining.

Continuous Underline (.UL ON/OFF)

Continuous underlining—underlining both the words and the spaces between them—is achieved by using the dot command .UL ON/OFF.

When you want continuous underlining, precede the text with .**UL ON**. Remember that the period (dot) goes in column 1, and no information but the command can be on the line. All underlining in the document following the dot command will be continuous unless .**UL OFF** is inserted at some point further along.

BOLDFACE ($^\wedge$PB)

Let's print the last two words of the document in Example 6A in boldface. Place the cursor over the first letter of the word *professional* and, with the insert mode on, press $^\wedge$**PB**. Position the cursor immediately after the period following *appearance*, and again press $^\wedge$**PB**. The words *professional appearance* are now bracketed by the symbols $^\wedge$B (depending on how the toggle is set) and displayed in boldface. The symbol $^\wedge$B signifies boldface. The symbols can be removed from the screen, as noted before, by selecting $^\wedge$**OD**. Notice that when the symbols are displayed on the screen, the line in which they appear extends past the right end of the ruler line; but since the $^\wedge$B's will not be printed, your printed document will still be right-justified. With the print display on, move the cursor several spaces to the left of the words *print functions* and, using the cursor controls, move the cursor one space at a time to the right. Watch the column number in the status line and notice that it does not change when the cursor crosses the $^\wedge$B symbols (just as it does not change when the cursor crosses lines containing dot commands). Normally, when you edit or enter a document, you want the print display off. There are times, though, as you'll see shortly, when viewing these symbols is useful.

ADDITIONAL PRINT FUNCTIONS

WordStar offers print functions to print strikeout, italics, double strike, subscripts, and superscripts. As you try each of these print functions, you will notice that each brackets the characters or text with different symbols, and in all cases the bracketed text display is highlighted. Again you will normally work with the print display off. However, when you are working with several print-display formats and are unsure what the highlighting represents, you can turn the print display on to view the symbols. Practice using these functions now, entering the command characters before and after the text you want to affect. Use a single file and then print it so you can see the appearance of the text.

Strikeout ($^\wedge$PX)

To use WordStar's strikeout capability, select $^\wedge$PX. On screen it appears as $^\wedge$XStrikeout$^\wedge$X, and when printed as

S̶t̶r̶i̶k̶e̶o̶u̶t̶

You may change the strikeout character from the default symbol , —, to some other character.

Change Strikeout Character (.XX)

To change the strikeout character, enter the dot command .XX followed by your new strikeout character. For example, entering .XX # will cause the previous example to print as

S#t#r#i#k#e#o#u#t

Italics (^PY)

To print a section of your file in italics place the cursor at the beginning of the section you want in italics and select ^PY. At the end of the section again select ^PY. On the screen the section bracketed will appear in bold.

Double Strike (^PD)

Double striking makes a word or phrase stand out; it does not print as dark as boldface.

Subscript (^PV)

Subscripts are most commonly used in equations.

Superscript (^PT)

Superscripts are used in equations and to indicate footnotes.

Not all printers can handle all of WordStar's special print functions. Check your printer manual if you have difficulty using any of these functions.

RIBBON COLOR (^P—)

If you work with a printer that offers a variety of print colors, you can easily select the color you wish. Place the cursor at the beginning of the section where the color is to change and select ^P—. The Colors window and options for your printer are displayed. An example follows.

Select the desired color. At the end of the section again use ^P— to return to the normal color. The color selected is displayed as a tag, <Light Blue>, in your file.

Caution: If you use a red-black ribbon, be sure the switch under the ribbon cartridge is set for red-black. When you switch back to multistrike ribbon, be sure to reset this switch, or you will get only half the use you should from your ribbon.

PRINT PAUSE (^PC)

At times you may find it convenient to pause while printing — maybe
to insert an envelope or to change print wheels. Typing ^**PC** places a
^C in a file so that printing will stop precisely where you want it to.
You can then change print wheels to insert special characters or italics
for a word or phrase. The code ^C also must be inserted at the end of
the special section so the printer will stop again to allow you to reinsert
the original print wheel. When the printer stops, "PRINT PAUSED"
will appear in the status line. Display the PRINTING dialog box
(select P from the File menu or ^KP from the Traditional menu) and
then press **C** to continue printing.

CHANGE PRINT DRIVER (^P?)

The letters or documents you enter in the computer with WordStar can
be printed on paper or saved (printed) on a disk. The software that
operates your printer or prints to a disk is called a driver. Most people
work with only one printer and, therefore, never have to change drivers. However, some of you may find it useful at times to change drivers
for one of the following reasons:

- More than one printer is available.

- Save a file and print it at another computer.

- Transfer a file to WordStar 4 format.

- View file format on screen before printing.

To view the list of printer drivers available, select ^**P?**. The display
on your screen will, of course, depend on the printers you have
installed. An example follows.

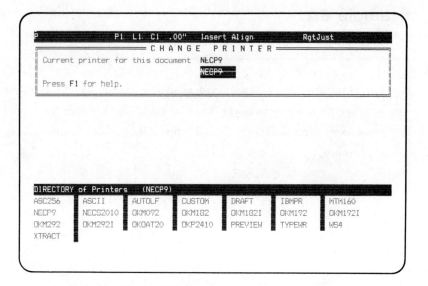

Use the arrow keys to make your selection and press ENTER.

WS4 is the driver used to translate your file into a format usable by WordStar 4.

EXERCISES

1. Enter Example 6B using the appropriate print functions so that when you print it, your printout looks the same as the example.

2. Edit the exercise you typed for Lesson 5, changing the high school name and address to boldface and the words *Requirements* and *Example* to double strike.

3. Use WordStar's subscript and superscript print enhancements to print the equation below.

$$y = a_1 x^2 + a_2 x + a_3$$

Example 6A

The print functions are listed near the bottom of the command sheet. In some documents they are not only necessary but, when used appropriately, give your work a very professional appearance.

Example 6B

```
Mr. Bob Harris

    AV INVENTORY - SCHOOL CODE

As you requested, the following is school identification by code.

                    1..........Martinez Elementary

                    2..........John Swett

                    3..........Las Juntas

                    4..........Martinez Junior High

                    5..........District Office

                    6..........Adult School

                    7..........Trailer

                    8..........Alhambra High School
```

CALCULATOR MODE
SHORTHAND MODE

This lesson introduces two operations that are not common in word processors but can be very useful: the capability to transfer to calculator mode while editing and the capability to create and use macros (a macro is a combination of commands that can be executed by a single command).

In calculator mode, you can interrupt the editing process, solve a math problem, return to your editing, and with a command, place the result of your calculation in your file. Calculator mode also allows you to add numbers while editing.

Macros allow you to streamline the command-entry process. You can create macros for frequently used command combinations so you can later implement them by pressing only two keys. You create macros using shorthand mode.

CALCULATOR MODE (^QM)

To try these ideas, open a file using Speed Write. While working with a WordStar file you can transfer to the Calculator menu and perform calculations using any of the 14 mathematical operators displayed. Press ^QM (or select it from the "Other" menu by pressing ALT-O to view that menu) and your screen displays

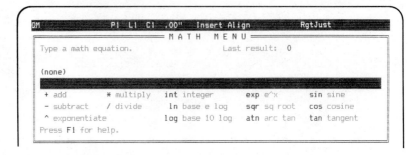

WordStar follows standard mathematical procedures in evaluating the formulas you enter. In general, operations are evaluated from left to right in order of precedence. Table 7-1 shows the order of precedence.

The order of precedence can be changed by placing parentheses around the operations you want to take place first. If parentheses are grouped one pair within another, the innermost grouping is evaluated first. For a more detailed review of this process, consult a book on algebra or BASIC programming. Let's solve a problem. We'll find the amount of interest due on a loan during one month. The formula for interest is

Interest = principal × rate × time

Use this data:

principal = $14,364.71

rate = 11.5%

time = 1 month or 1/12 of a year

Operator	Operation	Order
^	Exponentiation	Highest
*,/	Multiplication, division	Middle
+,−	Addition, subtraction	Lowest

TABLE 7-1   Order of Precedence

Select ^QM to display the Math menu. The cursor is in the formula line ready to accept your entry. Enter **14364.71∗.115/12**. Press ENTER, and the result is displayed following "Last result:" in the upper-right corner of the menu.

Note that the multiplication symbol is an asterisk. The asterisk is universally used with computers to represent multiplication.

At this point you can modify the formula either by making corrections or by entering new values. Use editing keys as you normally would in a document. At any time you can press ^**R** to replace the edited formula with the original that is displayed above the formula field. Pressing ENTER again produces the results for the new entries. To transfer results to the document you are editing, you must switch to shorthand mode, which will be discussed after a brief look at the other mathematical operators.

The int (integer) function eliminates the decimal portion of a number. To see how this works, press ^**R** to return the interest formula to the formula line. With insert mode on, edit the formula to read int(14364.71∗.115/12) and press ENTER. The result is 137. Note that it does not round the number to the nearest whole number, but eliminates the decimal portion of fractions (for example, int(9.1) and int(9.9) both equal 9).

In each of the remaining functions, the number you provide as the argument must be enclosed in parentheses. Consult appropriate reference books if your work involves this type of material. A simple example of how values are written for each function is shown in Example 7A at the end of this lesson.

Math mode gives results to 14 decimal places. For convenience, in Example 7A the samples with the ellipses have been shortened to three decimal places. If WordStar's calculator can't handle a formula you provide, the program will ask you to check the formula.

The other function of the calculator mode, adding numbers in your document, is discussed in Lesson 8, when blocking is introduced.

SHORTHAND MODE (ESC)

Besides offering an extensive assortment of built-in commands, WordStar allows you to create new commands by combining existing commands in different ways. You do this using macros created using shorthand mode.

Shorthand mode provides three things: a set of built-in macros that cannot be modified, a set of built-in macros that can be modified, and the capability to create new macros. You display the Shorthand menu by pressing the ESC key. Press ESC and the screen displays

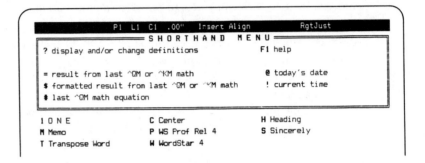

The ? on the first line of the Shorthand menu allows you to define your own macros, as you'll see shortly. Pressing ^ F1 provides help about how to use the Shorthand menu.

The remaining symbols in the Shorthand menu are built-in commands — the macros that cannot be modified. Those below the menu are macros supplied by WordStar that *can* be modified or even eliminated. This is also the area where macros you create are displayed. All macros, whether built in or user created, are executed by pressing two keys: ESC plus one other key.

The macros you create will depend on the type of work you do. What is appropriate for one person may be completely useless to another. First let's look at the built-in macros, then at the ones provided by WordStar, and finally at creating some representative examples of new macros.

FIXED BUILT-IN MACROS

WordStar provides the following built-in macros:

Keys	Action
ESC =	Prints the last result obtained in calculator mode (^QM) or block mode (^KM) (we'll examine ^KM in the next lesson)

Keys	Action
ESC #	Prints the last equation entered in calculator mode
ESC $	Prints the last result obtained in calculator mode in dollar format
ESC @	Prints today's date in your document (provided the date is set correctly in the computer)
ESC !	Prints the correct time (provided the time is set correctly in the computer)

To try these macros, open a file with the name EXAMPLE.7B. Then press ^QM, enter the interest equation presented earlier, and then press ^U to return to the file. Enter Example 7B, shown at the end of this lesson, pressing the ESC key each time the word *Esc* appears in the example. Your screen should be similar to this:

```
The interest on your loan is due today,

January 9, 1987.  It is now 4:24 PM and

I have not yet received your payment.

The amount due is $137.66, to be more

precise 137.661804167.  The result was

arrived at by using the following

equation:  14364.71*.115/12.
```

USER-DEFINED BUILT-IN MACROS (ESC?)

The built-in macros that you can modify are accessed from the Shorthand menu. Press ESC to display the Shorthand menu, followed by the ? key, and the screen displays

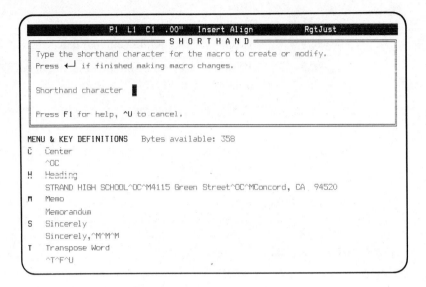

```
        P1  L1  C1   .00"   Insert Align              RgtJust
                      ═══ S H O R T H A N D ═══
  Type the shorthand character for the macro to create or modify.
  Press ↵ if finished making macro changes.

  Shorthand character  █

  Press F1 for help, ^U to cancel.


  MENU & KEY DEFINITIONS    Bytes available: 358
  C   Center
      ^OC
  H   Heading
      STRAND HIGH SCHOOL^OC^M4115 Green Street^OC^MConcord, CA  94520
  M   Memo
      Memorandum
  S   Sincerely
      Sincerely,^M^M^M
  T   Transpose Word
      ^T^F^U
```

Three items of information are displayed for each macro:

- The letter (shorthand character) you press with ESC to invoke the macro

- The description of the macro as displayed in the main Shorthand menu

- The WordStar definition that make up the macro

For example, to invoke centering, you press ESC and **C** (the screen description of this macro is Center) and the macro invokes the definition ^OC.

This macro saves only one keystroke: Pressing the two keys ESC and C produces the same result as pressing the three keys ^, O, and C. Other macros save many keystrokes.

Try each of these macros to see their effect. Look back at the definition in the Shorthand menu to see if the command does what you expected.

DESIGNING YOUR OWN MACROS

In addition to using WordStar's built-in commands, you can create your own. For example, you can create a macro to enter a common phrase or name that you type frequently during your work day. To see how you do this, let's create a macro to enter the phrase "Martinez Unified School District." Again display the Shorthand menu and press **?**.

You are going to enter a new macro now so you need to prepare by determining the three items of information you will need.

1. The letter (shorthand character) you will use to invoke the macro (character to be defined)

2. The macro description (for the Esc menu)

3. The commands that WordStar uses to carry out the macro (definition)

For your first item try to use a letter that will help you remember what the macro does. In this case, since the first letter of our expression *M* is used for another macro, let's use the last letter of Martinez, *Z*, in response to "Shorthand character". Enter **Z** and the screen displays the SHORT-HAND dialog box shown below.

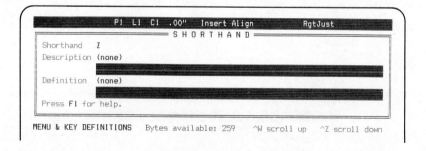

```
       P1  L1  C1  .00"   Insert Align         RgtJust
                    = S H O R T H A N D =
  Shorthand   Z
  Description (none)


  Definition  (none)


  Press F1 for help.

MENU & KEY DEFINITIONS   Bytes available: 259   ^W scroll up  ^Z scroll down
```

In the Description field enter **MUSD**, and in the Definition field enter **Martinez Unified School District**. Press ENTER.

WordStar now returns to the initial question, "Shorthand character". You can now enter another macro or exit. To exit, press ENTER. The question "Store macro changes on disk (Y/N)?", is displayed. Enter **Y**, the macro is saved, and WordStar immediately returns to Edit Mode. (If you enter **N**, the macro is only retained in memory for the current editing session.) Press ESC **Z** and "Martinez Unified School District" is displayed on the screen. If a macro of this type is inserted in the text of an existing file, the paragraph will be automatically reformatted.

Let's try a variation of this macro that has two differences. First it contains control codes (the CTRL key is used) and second the definition of the macro is longer than will fit on the definition line.

To enter control codes in a macro, press ^P prior to the control code you want. For example, to use centering in a macro enter ^P^OC before the data to be centered. The second modification occurs because the definition we'll use is longer than the definition line. Let's enter the Strand High School letterhead shown in Example 4B. You're entering a heading for a letter, so enter **H** as the Shorthand character and **Heading** as the description. The definition line has room for 62 characters. If your entry is longer than this, as it is here, you must enter the last portion first. In this case, enter the phone number; move the cursor back to the beginning of the definition line and, with insert on, enter the name, address, state, and ZIP code. The phone number is pushed off the screen, but don't worry about that. The data you type is shown here. Be sure to follow the screen instructions and precede control commands with ^P.

```
STRAND HIGH SCHOOL^P^OC^P^M415 Green Street^P^OC^P^M
Concord, CA  94520^P^OC^P^M(415) 798-5209^P^OC^P^M
```

The following portion of your entry is displayed on the shorthand definition line:

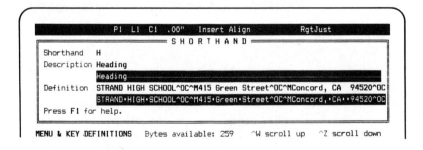

Again the phone number is pushed off the screen to the right. Return to the document, press ESC-H, and your screen displays

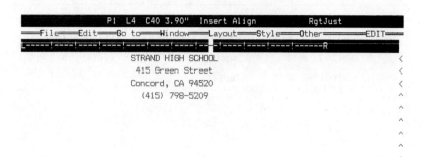

As a final example, here's a macro that prints x^2 when ESC-X is pressed. Enter the definition as x^P^PT2^P^PT. Note that in order to enter a CTRL sequence as a shorthand macro, you must type CTRL-P before every character that you want WordStar to interpret as a command. If you do not do this, WordStar will simply insert the characters in the document and will not treat them as commands.

Some additional macros will be introduced in later lessons.

EXERCISES

1. Modify WordStar's built-in macro that prints "sincerely" followed by three carriage returns so that it concludes with your name, as in this example:

    Sincerely,

    John Smith

2. Write a macro to move the cursor to the space after the last letter of a word (instead of to the first letter of the next word, as CTRL-→ does).

Example 7A

```
ln(10) = .693...    exp(3) = 20.085...  atn(1) = 45

log(100) = 2        sqr(64) = 8         sin(45) = .707...

cos(60) = .5        tan(45) = 1
```

Example 7B

```
The interest on your loan is due today,
Esc@.  It is now Esc! and I have not yet
received payment.  The amount due is
$Esc$, to be more precise Esc=.  The
result was arrived at by using the
following equation:  Esc#.
```

MOVE AND COPY BLOCK COMMANDS WINDOW COMMANDS COLUMN COMMANDS

Block commands allow you to perform several functions that are not possible with a standard typewriter. Rather than having to work with single characters, words, or lines of text, with blocks you can manipulate larger sections of text.

The block applications used in the beginning of this lesson may be accessed with the traditional WordStar commands shown in each section or they may be selected from the Edit menu.

MOVING BLOCKS (^KB, ^KK, ^KV)

Load your EXAMPLE.1 file. With insert mode on, place the cursor at the beginning of the file, over the *M* in *Most,* and type ^KB. The symbols <B> appear on the screen in reverse video, and *Most* will have moved three spaces to the right. Move the cursor to the end of the first paragraph, after the period, and type $^\wedge$**KK**. The blocked material appears in reverse video. Note also that a B now appears in the flag column at the beginning of the block, and a K now appears in the flag column at the end of the block.

Move the cursor to the end of the file by pressing $^\wedge$END and press ENTER. Type $^\wedge$**KV**, and the highlighted paragraph is moved to where the cursor is positioned.

Place the cursor back at the beginning of the file and again type $^\wedge$**KV**. The paragraph is returned to its original position. With this command you can move a phrase, sentence, paragraph, or page to any position in the document. Just place the cursor at the position where you want the blocked material to be moved and type $^\wedge$**KV**. Try this now by interchanging paragraphs 1 and 2. A block remains defined until another block is specified.

The size of the block you wish to move is limited by the amount of memory available in the computer. If you try to move too large a block, you will be informed by the message "Block too long." You can then divide your material into two or three smaller sections and move them one at a time.

COPYING BLOCKS ($^\wedge$KC)

Instead of moving a block of material from one place to another, you may want to copy some text but not have it removed from its original position. To do this, mark the material in the same manner as before, move the cursor to the position for the new text, and type $^\wedge$**KC**. This copies the blocked material at the position of the cursor and also leaves the material in its original position.

To mark a different section, move the cursor to the beginning of the new section and type $^\wedge$**KB** and then move the cursor to the end of the section and type $^\wedge$**KK**. The symbols B and K in the flag column now bracket the new section and no longer appear in the previous block. You can change the blocked section as often as you like.

To eliminate the highlighting from the screen display, type $^\wedge$**KH**. Normal video returns, and the B and K in the flag column can no longer be seen, although their position will be remembered for the remainder of the editing session or until another block of text is marked. Type $^\wedge$**KH** again, and they will reappear—try it.

BLOCKING COLUMNS
ON/OFF (^KN)

To block columns of data, you must turn on column mode. Select ^KN from the Edit menu or type ^K and choose option N from the menu displayed. This changes the block-moving capabilities of WordStar to column mode.

Enter the first portion of Example 8A. (*Note:* Enter only the first row and use the block commands to copy in the next four rows.) Now using column mode, move the columns to duplicate the pattern shown in section (2) of the example. You can do this with two block moves. Now produce section (3).

You can move or copy not only columns of characters but also columns of spaces, as was done in section (4) of this example. This can be a very useful application when you have a long file with columns of names or numbers and you wish to change the spacing. To do this, you mark off a column of spaces, and copy it to a new position, just as you would text.

REPLACING COLUMNS (^KI)

You no doubt noticed that when you copy or move a column of material, any data that occupied the area to which you moved material or any data to the right is moved further to the right the same number of spaces that the column is wide. You can stop this situation from occurring by using the Column Replace command, ^KI. Column Replace can be invoked only if column mode is already turned on. With column mode on, select ^KI. Notice in the status line that "Column" changes to "ColRepl." Use Example 8A to experiment and familiarize yourself with the ^KI command. Using ^KI, create pattern (5). A final note: Pressing ^U (Undo) restores the block of data most recently deleted by Column Replace.

USING WINDOWS

So far you have worked with one file while editing. WordStar has the capability of displaying and allowing you to have two files open at the same time. The screen is divided or split into two sections, called *windows,* where you work with the files being edited.

To look at the window commands, press ALT-W. The Window menu is open as shown below.

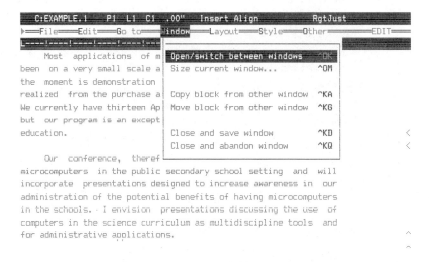

First, let's go through each of the commands and then we'll open a couple of files to try each command.

Open/Switch Windows (^OK)

The command $^\wedge$OK has a dual function: first, to open another window if only one is open; and second, if two windows are open, to switch the cursor from one window to the other. Whichever window the cursor is in is the active window, allowing you to edit the file displayed.

Window Size (^OM)

When a second window is open, WordStar automatically allocates half of the screen for editing the second file—eleven lines for the first file (top window), and ten lines for the second file (bottom window). When you open a second file, it may be to edit one of the existing files on your disk, or it may simply be a new file.

To change the size of the window, move the cursor to that window and select the command ^OM. You are given the number of lines in the window and asked: "Length of Window." Enter the size in number of lines. The number of lines available in the Edit window will be one less than the number you enter. If you enter 0 (zero) as the size for your window, the other file will become active with the full screen available. The other file is still open and you can still switch between the two open files with ^OM.

Move/Copy Blocks Between Windows (^KA, ^KG)

Just as you can move and copy blocks within a file, you can also move or copy blocks between files displayed in different windows. To copy or move blocked material from one file to another, use the command ^KA to copy and ^KG to move the block.

The steps to move or copy a block of material between windows are outlined below.

1. Move the cursor to the window containing the material you want to move or copy.

2. Using ^KB and ^KK, mark the desired block.

3. Move the cursor to the other window by selecting ^OK.

4. Position the cursor where you want the moved or copied block material to begin.

5. Select ^KG to move or ^KA to copy the material.

As an example, look at the following illustration.

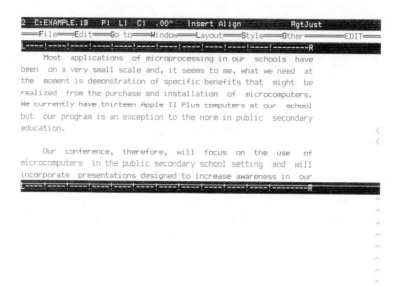

```
2 C:EXAMPLE.1B   P1  L1  C1   .00"   Insert Align          RgtJust
====File====Edit====Go to====Window====Layout====Style====Other====EDIT====
----!----!----!----!----!----!----!----!----!----!----!--------R
     Most  applications  of microprocessing in our  schools have
been  on a very small scale and, it seems to me, what we need  at
the  moment is demonstration of specific benefits that  might  be
realized  from the purchase and installation  of  microcomputers.
We currently have thirteen Apple II Plus computers at our  school
but  our program is an exception to the norm in public  secondary
education.

     Our  conference,  therefore,  will  focus  on  the  use   of
microcomputers  in the public secondary school setting  and  will
incorporate  presentations designed to increase awareness in  our
----!----!----!----!----!----!----!----!----!----!----!--------R
```

For this illustration EXAMPLE.1 of Lesson 1 is used. Window 2 was opened with the name EXAMPLE.1B. Notice in the status line that on the left is displayed "2 C:EXAMPLE 1B." The 2 tells you that window 2 is the active window and, of course, the rest is the drive and the file name. If the Switch Windows command ($^\wedge$OK) were entered, the number 1, for window 1, and the name of the new active file, EXAMPLE.1, would appear there.

SAVING WITH TWO FILES OPEN

The commands to save when two edit windows are open are the same as those used when one file is open. As you might expect, there are some minor differences in their function. Starting with $^\wedge$KQ and $^\wedge$KD, let's consider each save command that displays in the Window window.

$^\wedge$KD   Saves the active file, closes its window, and makes the file in the other window active.

$^\wedge$KQ   Abandons the active file, closes its window, and makes the remaining file active.

$^\wedge$KS   Same as with a single window open (saves the file and returns the cursor to its same position in the file where you can resume editing).

$^\wedge$KX   Saves the active file. closes its window, and makes the file in the other window active (same as $^\wedge$KD).

Try each of these operations. Open EXAMPLE.1. Now select $^\triangle$OK to open a second window. When asked to name the file, enter the name EXAMPLE.1A.

EXERCISES

1. Type five names and addresses with different ZIP codes (one name per line). Using the Block commands, rearrange the names and addresses so they are in alphabetical order.

2. Rearrange the names and addresses in exercise 1 so they are in order by ZIP code from smallest to longest.

3. Enter Example 8B. Using Block commands, arrange the questions in reverse order.

4. Enter Example 8C. Forms of one type or another are easy to create with WordStar by using the Block commands. Set the ruler line and tabs to conform to this example and enter the form as far as the B on the right side. (Do *not* enter the A or the B.) With the cursor at the position of the B, type $^\wedge$**KK**. Move the cursor to the position of the A in the example and type $^\wedge$**KB**. Move the cursor to the end of the file (the position of the C) and type $^\wedge$**KC**. Move the cursor back to position A and again type $^\wedge$**KB**. Return to the end of the file and type $^\wedge$**KC**. By repeating this process you will move progressively larger blocks of material. Keep an eye on the line number in the status line so that you don't go past the end of the page.

5. Try moving blocked material from one window to another. Open Example 8B from exercise 3. Open a second window using a new file name, TEST.PHY. Copy the heading plus questions 2, 4-6, and 8 to window 2. Save each file and open each again to verify that Example.8B is unchanged and TEST.PHY contains the data you transferred.

Example 8A

```
(1)
AAAAA   BBBBB   CCCCC   11111   22222   33333
AAAAA   BBBBB   CCCCC   11111   22222   33333
AAAAA   BBBBB   CCCCC   11111   22222   33333
AAAAA   BBBBB   CCCCC   11111   22222   33333
AAAAA   BBBBB   CCCCC   11111   22222   33333

(2)
11111   22222   33333   AAAAA   BBBBB   CCCCC
11111   22222   33333   AAAAA   BBBBB   CCCCC
11111   22222   33333   AAAAA   BBBBB   CCCCC
11111   22222   33333   AAAAA   BBBBB   CCCCC
11111   22222   33333   AAAAA   BBBBB   CCCCC

(3)
11111   AAAAA   22222   BBBBB   33333   CCCCC
11111   AAAAA   22222   BBBBB   33333   CCCCC
11111   AAAAA   22222   BBBBB   33333   CCCCC
11111   AAAAA   22222   BBBBB   33333   CCCCC
11111   AAAAA   22222   BBBBB   33333   CCCCC

(4)
11111      AAAAA      22222      BBBBB      33333      CCCCC
11111      AAAAA      22222      BBBBB      33333      CCCCC
11111      AAAAA      22222      BBBBB      33333      CCCCC
11111      AAAAA      22222      BBBBB      33333      CCCCC
11111      AAAAA      22222      BBBBB      33333      CCCCC

(5)
AAAAA   BBBBB   CCCCC   11111   22222   33333
AAAAA   BAAAB   CAAAC   1AAA1   2AAA2   3AAA3
AAAAA   BAAAB   CAAAC   1AAA1   2AAA2   3AAA3
AAAAA   BAAAB   CAAAC   1AAA1   2AAA2   3AAA3
AAAAA   BBBBB   CCCCC   11111   22222   33333

        BBB     CCC     111     222     333
        BBB     CCC     111     222     333
        BBB     CCC     111     222     333
```

Example 8B

```
                      PHYSICS TEST

                      Chapters 7-8

Name_____        Period_____


1.   If  a small planet were discovered whose distance  from  the
     sun  was 16 times that of the earth, how many  times  longer
     than   the earth takes would the new planet take  to  circle
     the sun?

2.   The radius of the moon's orbit is 60 times greater than  the
     radius  of  the  earth.   How  many  times  greater  is  the
     acceleration  of  a  falling  body  on  the  earth than  the
     acceleration of the moon toward the earth?

3.   At what height above the earth's surface will a rocket  have
     1/4 the force of gravitation on it that it would have at sea
     level?  Express your answer in earth radii.

4.   A  75-kg  boy  stands  1  meter  away  from a 65-kg  girl.
     Calculate  the  force of attraction (gravitational) between
     them.

5.   If  you push a body with a force of 4 newtons for  1/2  sec,
     what impulse do you give the body?

6.   What  average  force  is necessary to stop a hammer  with  25
     newton-sec momentum in .05 sec?

7.   What  happens  to the momentum of a car when it comes  to  a
     stop?

8.   What  is  the kinetic energy of a 2-kg hammer moving  at  20
     m/sec?
```

Example 8C

```
                         COMPUTER CENTER LOG

|JOB DESCRIPTION                    |IN-DATE | FROM |OUT-DATE|  TO  |
A------------------------------------|--------|------|--------|------|
|-----------------------------------|--------|------|--------|------|
|                                   |        |      |        |     B|
C-----------------------------------|--------|------|--------|------|
|-----------------------------------|--------|------|--------|------|
|-----------------------------------|--------|------|--------|------|
|-----------------------------------|--------|------|--------|------|
|-----------------------------------|--------|------|--------|------|
|-----------------------------------|--------|------|--------|------|
|-----------------------------------|--------|------|--------|------|
|-----------------------------------|--------|------|--------|------|
|-----------------------------------|--------|------|--------|------|
|-----------------------------------|--------|------|--------|------|
|-----------------------------------|--------|------|--------|------|
|-----------------------------------|--------|------|--------|------|
|-----------------------------------|--------|------|--------|------|
|-----------------------------------|--------|------|--------|------|
|-----------------------------------|--------|------|--------|------|
|-----------------------------------|--------|------|--------|------|
|-----------------------------------|--------|------|--------|------|
|-----------------------------------|--------|------|--------|------|
```

Read, Write, Delete Blocks, Move to Beg/End Block Case Conversion Adding Within Blocks Set Marks

The previous lesson covered many of the block commands used by WordStar. Additional block commands are described in this lesson.

DELETE BLOCK (^KY)

Load Example 8B and block off question 3. Type ^**KY**; the entire block is deleted. This is an easy way to delete large sections of material.

Just as you can undo other delete commands, you can also undo block operations, *provided the block is not too large*. WordStar will advise you if the marked block is too large for the Undo command to restore and, if it is, will ask if the block should be deleted anyway.

WRITE BLOCK (^KW)

The Write Block command is used to take material entered in the file being edited and write it into a file on the disk. Suppose you have a paragraph or section of a report that is to be used in several different documents. The first time you type it, block it off and type ^KW.

The WRITE BLOCK dialog box is displayed. Enter the filename you wish to use to store the file on the disk. Press ENTER and the blocked material is saved on the disk.

If you use a name already on your disk or logged subdirectory, WordStar will inform you and ask: "Overwrite or Append (Y/N/A)?" Type

Y   To select Overwrite, which will completely replace the contents of the disk file with the blocked material

N   Select N and you return to the file being edited

A   To add the blocked material to the end of the disk file

READ FILE (^KR)

The Read File command is used to take material from the disk and add it to the file you are editing. This is similar to moving a block of material from one file to another when you have two windows open. The difference is that you are inserting a complete file, not just the blocked portion of a file. To try this, place the cursor where you want to add the material from the disk and type ^KR; WordStar will display the INSERT A FILE dialog box. After you supply the name, press ENTER, and the material from the disk will be inserted in the file you are editing at the position of the cursor. Your disk file is left intact.

Let's try this now with one of the questions in Example 8B. Block off the question. Type ^KW, enter a new file name, and press ENTER. Type ^KY to delete the question from the file you are editing. To reinsert the question, place the cursor where you want the question to appear and type ^KR and the file name under which you saved the question. Press ENTER and the question is back in place.

In addition to reading in files that are created using WordStar, you may use ^KR to read in files created using MailList and most versions of Lotus, Quattro, Symphony, and dBase. Once files or portions of files are read into WordStar, you may use all of WordStar editing features to modify the file. When reading a file, whether created using WordStar or another program, be sure to enter the appropriate path if the file is not on the logged subdirectory.

Keep in mind the following observations when reading in a spreadsheet file.

- To prevent realignment of column material, let .AW OFF precede the data being read into your WordStar file.

- Be sure the section of your file is in a nonproportional font where the spreadsheet is to be inserted.

- A dialog box will be displayed allowing you to select the desired spreadsheet range.

- Pressing ENTER, without modifying the range, selects the entire spreadsheet.

- If range names are used in a spreadsheet, they will be displayed and can be used to select the range.

DELETE FILE (^KJ)

To clear the disk of an unnecessary file, you can use ^KJ. To try this command, we will get rid of the file used to save the question in the previous example. Type ^**KJ** and the Delete window is displayed along with the directory. Enter the filename to delete and press ENTER. Press ^**KJ** again to display the directory and to verify that the file you deleted is no longer there.

While you have the directory on the screen, note that there are several files with the extension (the part after the period) BAK. This occurs each time you save a file after it is first saved. The most recently edited version will have the name you gave it with the extension you gave it, if any. The previous version will have the extension BAK, which stands for backup file.

The Delete File command can come in handy, particularly if you use a floppy drive system. Suppose you type a long document, attempt to save it by typing ^KD, and get the message "Disk full." This would be very frustrating if there weren't two possible solutions. First, check the directory and see if there are any backup files you can delete or perhaps a file that you no longer need (but don't exit to the opening menu to do this). If you see any unneeded files, select ^KJ to get rid of them. If you wish to check the files on another subdirectory, use ^KL to change that subdirectory. The second possibility, if you are using floppy disks, is to place a floppy disk with plenty of space in another drive, block off your file, and write it to the other drive. To do this, use the prefix for the new drive (for example, B:) to start the name of the file. If the file is long, you may need to execute the ^KW command more than once. Be sure to use the Append option each time you write a block to the disk file.

RETURN TO DOS (^KF)

Yet another solution to a full disk is to enter ^KF and return to DOS. There you can use the DOS ERASE command with the wild card option to quickly delete your BAK files. When command execution is complete, pressing any key returns you to WordStar.

Of course, the easiest approach is to check your disk before you start your work to make sure that there is sufficient room for your file.

MOVE TO BEGINNING/END OF BLOCK (^QB, ^QK)

With a block marked off, you can quickly move to the beginning or end of the block with the commands ^QB (to the beginning) and ^QK (to the end). Try these with a marked block in the current example. These commands are most useful with large blocks or with large files when the cursor is some distance (several pages) away from the block. These two commands are also options on the Go To menu.

CHANGING TO UPPERCASE/LOWERCASE (^K″, ^K′, ^K.)

You can change a blocked section of a file to all uppercase letters or all lowercase letters. Type ^K″ to change the block to all uppercase and ^K′ to change the block to all lowercase. Try this using EXAMPLE. 1, changing one paragraph to uppercase and the other to lowercase.

To change the blocked section back to the original format use ^K. (the period here is part of the command, not a punctuation mark). The command ^K. changes everything to lowercase except the letter following a period. In general this works quite well but occasionally there are difficulties, as in the preceding sentence where a period is used in a context other than to end a sentence. A more common example of this is when a period is used in an abbreviation such as e.g. or etc. You will also have to check the section when this command is applied to see if any proper nouns were used. In this case, you can also abandon the file to change back to its original format.

ADDING WITHIN BLOCKS (^KM)

WordStar will sum numbers in a blocked section of your file if you type ^KM. It does not make any difference whether the numbers are in a column or interspersed with text in a document. Press ^KM to determine and store the result; then press ESC= or ESC $ to print the result in your file. Some simple examples of numbers summed by using the ^KM command are shown here.

Sample	Comments
5 6 7 8 = 26	A single space is sufficient to separate numbers.
5,6,7,8 = 5678	A comma between numbers is not a proper separator, so the numbers are not added.
5, 6, 7, 8 = 26	A comma plus a space does properly separate numbers.

Sample	Comments
−5 6 7 8 = 16	A hyphen before a number is considered a minus sign.
−5 6 (7) 8 = 2	A number enclosed in parenthesis is also evaluated as a negative number.
3e3 6e3 = 9000	Numbers may be entered using exponential notation.

ROUNDING TO THE NEAREST PENNY

Dollar format also may be used at any time. Dollar format does not round to the nearest penny. If rounding is a factor to be considered in your work, use the Shorthand menu to enter this macro:

^K B^[= .005^KK^KM^[^KY^[$

Note that the symbols ^[represent the ESC key. The commands in this macro are outlined in the following illustration.

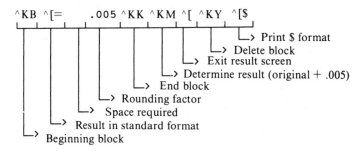

SET MARKS (^K0-9)

In multiple-page documents it is useful to set *marks* at appropriate intervals so that you can quickly go to any part of the document. Ten such marks can be set (0-9). Although these marks are not particularly useful with a short file, to try them we will set some in Example 8B. There is no point in putting a mark at the beginning or end of a file because WordStar provides commands to move to these positions. Let's place the first mark at question 1. Place the cursor in column 1 before the number 1 and type ^**K0**. The symbols <0> will appear. Move the cursor to question 2, column 1, and type ^**K1**. Continue in this manner until you have entered the appropriate symbols next to each question.

Now when you type ^**Q** and one of the integers 0 through 9, the cursor will move to the proper mark—try it. Again, this procedure is most useful for long documents.

EXERCISES

1. Load EXAMPLE.1. Block off the first half and write it to the disk. Do the same with the second half (using a new name).

2. Using the Block Read command, rejoin the two files you separated in exercise 1.

3. Using the Delete File command, delete the two files you created in exercise 1 from the disk.

4. Delete all backup and other unwanted files from your disk or subdirectory. From WordStar, examine the files on other disks or subdirectories and delete those not needed. (Be sure to keep one copy of each example.)

5. Use block addition to verify all the sums in Example 9A.

Example 9A

```
                                         Year Ended December 88

                                          1988            1987
                                       -----------------------------
Sales, less returns and allowances     $89,731,224     $81,427,649
Other income                               743,012         677,111
                                         ----------      ----------
                                        90,474,236      82,104,760

Costs and expenses
  Cost of goods sold                    68,447,490      60,251,113
  Selling, general and administrative
    expenses                            15,096,582      13,934,948
  Other expenses                           766,831         737,417
  State and Federal income taxes         3,005,624       3,760,089
                                         ----------      ----------

    Total costs and expenses            87,316,527      78,683,559
                                         ==========      ==========
Net income before extraordinary items
    of income or expense                 3,157,709       3,421,201
Add or (deduct) extraordinary items
    of income or expense (net of
    related income tax $367,807)          (385,862)          -
                                         ----------      ----------
Net income                             $ 2,771,847     $ 3,421,201
Earnings per share of common stock:
  Earnings before extraordinary item         $1.34           $1.44
  Extraordinary item                           .16             -
                                             -----           -----
Net earnings                                 $1.18           $1.44
                                             =====           =====
```

10

PRINT HEIGHT, WIDTH, AND LENGTH COMMANDS

This lesson is devoted mainly to commands that can affect the dimensions of your document. To a large extent, your ability and need to use the commands introduced in this lesson depend on the type of printer you are using.

In this lesson we will discuss the following commands:

Command	Function	Default Setting
.CW	Character width	12 (for standard pitch)
.LH	Line height (per inch)	8 (6 lines to the inch)
.PL	Paper length	66 lines (11 inches)
.PO	Page offset	8 columns (4/5 inch)
^PA	Alternate print pitch	Printer/User determined
^PN	Normal (default) pitch	Printer/User determined

Command	Function	Default Setting
$^\wedge$P =	Font selection	Printer/User determined
$^\wedge$Q =	Go to font	None (N/A)

The purpose of these dot commands is to change the default values for an individual file. When you get used to WordStar, you can change the default values so that the values you specify automatically take effect each time WordStar is loaded. This is done with the program WSCHANGE, discussed in Appendix C.

Remember, when entering the dot commands, that the dot must be entered in column 1, followed by a two-letter command (in either upper- or lowercase) and a value, if required.

Before we discuss these commands, review the following:

- The most common paper size is 8 1/2 x 11 inches.

- Typewriters print 10 (pica) or 12 (elite) characters per inch across the paper, 12 being the most common; 6 lines per inch are printed vertically.

- The screen you are working with has 80 columns. In most cases not all of these columns are used for text, because the ruler is usually set to a width less than 80.

LINE HEIGHT (.LH)

The Line Height command allows you to specify how many lines per inch are printed on a page (some printers cannot be controlled this way—find out whether yours can). Line height is specified in units of 1/48 of an inch. The default value is 8, or 8/48 of an inch, which reduces to 1/6, or six lines per inch. All of the examples you have printed so far have been printed using this default value.

Load Example 3 from Lesson 3 and print it at eight lines per inch. To enter the Line Height dot command, you may have to insert a blank line at the beginning of the file. Type **.LH 6.** The 6 tells you that the printer will scroll down 6/48, or 1/8, of an inch after each line is printed. Check the status line to be sure the dot is in column 1. Remember that you cannot have any file text on the same line as a dot command. Press CTRL-PRTSCR to save the file and print it. Check to see that your printer prints at eight lines per inch.

CHARACTER WIDTH (.CW)

The minimum movement for the character width command is 1/120 inch, a very small increment. The default value is 12 (12/120=1/10), or 10 characters per inch. To change this value, type a period in column 1, then CW, then a number representing the value you wish to use. For example, type **.CW 10** (10/120=1/12) to print 12 characters per inch. On some printers you cannot control the character width with the .CW command.

Another function of the CW command is to change fonts. Again, this is determined by your printer's capability. On many dot matrix printers, setting .CW 10 (1/12 inch) will select elite print and .CW 12 (1/10 inch) will select pica. Most newer dot matrix printers and laser printers offer a wide variety of font selection in this manner.

PAPER LENGTH (.PL)

Because the standard paper length is 11 inches and printers normally print six lines per inch, the default paper length value is 66. If you are using paper of a nonstandard length or if you change the line height you can change the number of lines that will print per page by entering that number after the .PL command.

Note that some laser printers use a default setting of 62 lines per page. Check your printer manual for more information.

PAGE OFFSET EVEN/ODD (.POO, .POE)

 The Page Offset command determines the left margin and has a default value of 8 (8/10, or 4/5, of an inch). This value is appropriate when you are using 10 pitch type and the default ruler line with a length of 65. If your file has particularly narrow or wide text, or if you are using 12 pitch, this value may need to be changed. Always use the .PO command to control where a file is printed on a sheet of paper, rather than changing the position of continuous-feed paper in the printer. Moving the paper and forgetting to return it to its original position is aggravating to the next user.

If you are preparing a document that will be bound or placed in some special type of folder, it may be appropriate to have the page offset different for the odd and even pages. Use the page offset commands .POO (odd) or .POE (even) to set the offset separately for odd and even pages. There cannot be a space between the .PO and the letters O, for odd, or E, for even. .POE .5″ would set the even pages to .5 inch or 1/2 inch. .POO .8″ would set the odd pages to .8 inch. .PO 12 would set the offset for both even and odd to 12 columns.

To practice with this command, load the text from Example 1. Change the ruler line so the left margin is in column 1 and the right margin is in column 50. Reform the paragraphs to conform to this ruler line. Print the file so it is centered on the paper, using the following assumptions: The paper is 8 1/2 inches, or 85 columns, wide. The text is 50 columns wide, which leaves 35 columns to be used for the left and right margins; use 17 for the left margin and 18 for the right margin. At the top of your file type **.PO 17** (remember, no other text should be placed on this line). Save and print the file.

NORMAL/ALTERNATE PITCH SELECTION (^PN, ^PA)

^PN and ^PA give you a quick easy way to change your printing pitch. Again the capability depends on your printer and its installation. Let's consider its most common effect on the three general categories of printers.

Dot Matrix

Most of the newer dot matrix printers offer a variety of fonts. The standard installation for this type of printer is to have normal pitch set to 10 pitch and alternate pitch set to 12. Pressing ^**PA** places <ALTERNATE> on the screen. See the following illustration for an example.

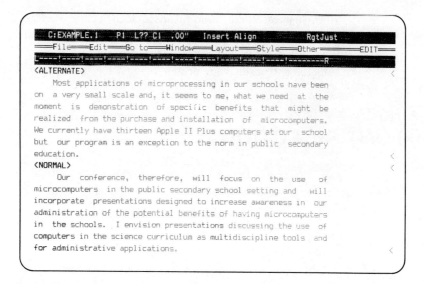

The default is normal pitch and doesn't show unless you enter ^**PN**. Usually this would only be done after a section was printed in alternate pitch. You can also use these commands to bracket a word or phrase for emphasis within a paragraph. The screen tags, normal and alternate, are toggled on and off using ^OD.

With appropriate use of the CW command, you can change the fonts associated with ^PN and ^PA as many times as you like in a file.

Daisy Wheel

You can use the same procedure with daisy wheel printers. These displays will be suppressed if ^OD or ^OP is in effect. In order to stop print to change the daisy wheel, enter ^**PC**, print pause (discussed in Lesson 6).

Laser Printer

Laser printers offer a wide variety of print fonts. You will have to determine what font is used for the alternate selection with your printer.

Note that on some laser printers, such as the Hewlett-Packard LaserJet, various type fonts are selected by changing character width settings. What fonts you can use are predetermined by the printer manufacturer. Consult your printer manual for more information.

FONT SELECTION (^P=)

If your printer has the capability of printing in a variety of fonts, you can easily change fonts within your document by selecting ^P=. A sample screen is displayed below. (Of course, what you have displayed will depend on the printer you have installed.)

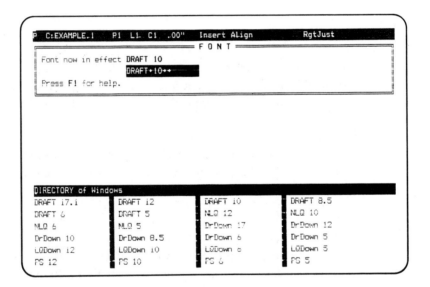

Select the desired font, using the arrow key, and press ENTER. You may bracket anything from a single character to a large portion of your file.

The distance indicator in the status line will keep track of the distance the cursor is from the left margin. Also, even if the font size changes and a variety of fonts are used in the same line, the printout will remain right justified. When a different font is selected, a font description or tag is displayed at the beginning of the section, as shown in the next screen. The font remains in effect until another font selection is made.

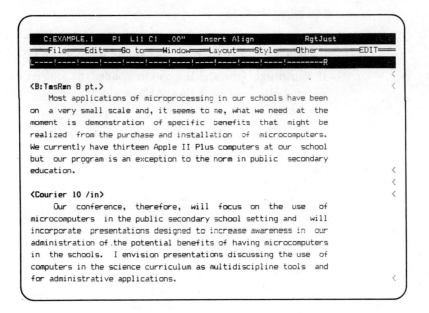

Go To Font (^Q=)

You can advance the cursor quickly to the next font flag in your file by selecting ^Q=. The search is from the position of the cursor toward the end of the file. To search the entire document place the cursor at the beginning of the file.

EXERCISES

1. Print a portion of one of your documents in alternate pitch. If you have a daisy wheel or thimble printer, use the Print Pause command (^PC) and change the print wheel to use both normal and alternate pitch.

2. On one of your large files, or one that comes with WordStar, use the odd/even offset to vary the margins for odd and even pages.

3. If your printer provides the option, change the font for different sections of one of your files. Also, select a word or phrase and change the font.

4. Use the Go to font command to quickly go through the file you used in Exercise 3 and change or remove the fonts you added there.

11

HEADER AND FOOTER DOT COMMANDS

In this lesson we will work with several more dot commands. These commands control what is printed at the top and bottom of each page. You should enter all header and footer dot commands at the beginning of your file, before entering any text. Use the following chart for reference.

Command	Controls	Default
.MT	margin top	3 lines (1/2 inch)
.HM	header margin	2 lines (1/3 inch)
.HE/.H1	header (first line)	Blank
.H2	header (second line)	Blank
.H3	header (third line)	Blank
.MB	margin bottom	8 lines (1 1/3 inches)

Command	Controls	Default
.FO/.F1	footer (first line)	Page number
.F2	footer (second line)	Blank
.F3	footer (third line)	Blank
.FM	footer margin	2 lines (1/3 inch; margin for page number)

The dot commands .HE and .FO (the letter O, not the number) are carryovers from earlier versions of WordStar. They allow headers and footers written by these earlier versions to be read by the current version. Note that you enter header and footer text on the same line as the dot command.

HEADERS (.HE/.H1, .H2, .H3)

The header commands are used to place text at the top of each page of a printed file. Any text typed after the header commands will be printed at the top of *each* new page in your printout. You can use up to three lines of header text. For the first header line you can use .HE or .H1. The second and third header lines must use .H2 and .H3, respectively.

DIFFERENT ODD/EVEN
HEADERS (.HEE, .HEO)

You may want to use different headers on odd and even pages, as is done in this book. To do this, add an o for odd and an e for even after the header command. As an example, the commands in the following illustration produced the headers for the manuscript copy of this lesson.

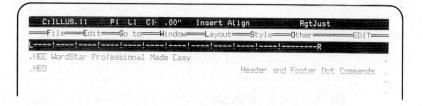

This same procedure applies to the footer commands discussed shortly.

Margin Top (.MT)

The .MT command has a default value of three lines. Normally, your printer is set at the top of the paper and, on screen, your text begins on line 1. When printing a file, the printer scrolls the paper up three lines before it begins to print. If this distance is not satisfactory, it can easily be changed by entering **.MT** and a number representing the number of lines you want the printer to scroll. This value can be either more or less than the default value. Another way to control the top margin, particularly for single-page documents, is to insert blank lines at the top of the file.

HEADER MARGIN (.HM)

The .HM command allows you to control the space between the header and the beginning of the file text. The value you give for the top margin (.MT) must be large enough to contain both the header and the header margin.

For example, note that the default value for the top margin (.MT) is 3, and the default value for the header margin (.HM) is 2. The difference between these values (3 − 2, or 1) is the number of lines available for the heading. To use all three header commands—.H1, .H2, and .H3—you can enter the commands **.MT 6** and **.HM 3**. The following figure illustrates this point.

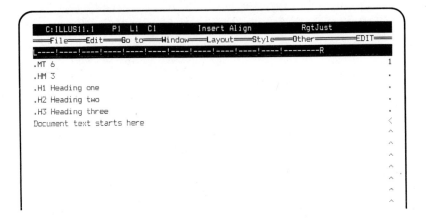

With the margin at the top set at 6 and the header margin set at 3, you have three lines available to enter header text. The following illustration shows the output from the previous illustration.

heading one
heading two
heading three

document text starts here

MARGIN BOTTOM (.MB)

The .MB command allows you to specify the number of lines for the bottom margin. The default value is 8, or 1 1/3 inches. Occasionally you will want to reduce this value so that you can fit another line or two of text on a page. You place this command, as well as the other commands controlling the bottom margin, at the beginning of your file.

FOOTERS (.FO/.F1, .F2, .F3)

The document page number is printed on the line controlled by .F1, but you can use the footer commands to automatically print any information you like at the foot of each page of your file. You have three lines for footing text. Again, the space available for footing comments is the difference between the bottom margin (.MB) and the footer margin (.FM). Using the default values, the difference is $8 - 2$, or 6, so you don't need to adjust the standard settings to take advantage of the three footer text lines.

FOOTER MARGIN (.FM)

The .FM command determines the space between your file text and the page number or footer text. Again, the spacing for the footer margin and the footer text must be included in the bottom margin command.

HEADERS AND FOOTERS

Two special format characters can be used with the header (.H1, .H2, .H3) and footer (.F1, .F2, .F3) commands.

\#   This symbol prints the current page number in place of the symbol. In a long document, the page number is automatically incremented and printed in the position of the # symbol. Other text may be included with the symbol in the footer. For example,

.F1 Chapter 6 - #

will print *Chapter 6* along with the appropriate page number in the footer of each page. The spaces between *.F1* and *Chapter 6* will be retained. If you have more than one chapter in the same file, you can enter a new footer command at the beginning of each chapter.

\   This symbol simply prints the next character (for example, \#
will print # instead of the page number; \ \ will print \).

When using headers and footers, note the following:

- To terminate headers or footers, you enter the header or footer
command without text on the page where you want the header or
footer to stop.

- You can enter a blank line between headers H1 and H3 by entering .H2 followed by two spaces and then pressing ENTER. Follow
the same procedure to enter a blank footer.

- Spaces entered between header or footer commands and the top
of the document text will be retained in printing.

- You can use bold, underline, and other print enhancements with
headers and footers just as you would in the standard text of a
document. With headers and footers the *commands* for the
enhancements, rather than the enhancements themselves, will be
displayed on the screen. Nevertheless, the enhancements will
appear on the printed copy.

- A maximum of 100 characters is normally allowed in a header or
footer. You can change this value by using WSCHANGE (see
Appendix C).

EXERCISES

1. Enter Example 11A using a ruler line with appropriate tabs (the
right margin is set to 75).

2. Use dot commands to print the file name and subdirectory name
in a header in Example 11A. Print the page number in a footer in
column 70.

3. Type Example 11B. Print Example 11B with page numbers at the
top of the page.

Example 11A

```
              VOCATIONAL EDUCATION STUDENT/COURSE INVENTORY


    Student Name_____ Sex_____/_____
                                         (male)  (female)


    Address_____ Telephone_____

           _____
                  (city)

    Grade Level_____ Birthdate_____/___/_____ LES Status_____


    Disadvantaged Status  Racial/Ethnic Code    Handicapped Status
       DISAD.ST.              R/E CODE             HNDCAP ST.
    --------------------  --------------------   --------------------


    (EC)____Economic     (AI) ____American Indian (MR)____Mentally Retarded
    (AC)____Academic               Alaskan Native (HH)____Hard of Hearing
                         (API)____Asian Pacific   (SI)____Speech Impaired
                                   Islander        (VH)____Visually Handi-
                         (BNH)____Black,                    capped
                                   Non-Hispanic   (ED)____Emotionally Dis-
                         (H)  ____Hispanic                  turbed
                         (F)  ____Filipino         (OHI)____Other Health Im-
                         (WNH)____White,                    paired
                                   Non-Hispanic   (MH)____Multi-handi-
                                                            capped
                                                  (SLD)____Specific Learn-
                                                            ing Disabled


              VOCATIONAL EDUCATION PROGRAM PRESENTLY ENROLLED



    I  Office Occupations                  II  Industrial Arts
    _____               _____
    (AC)____Accounting & Computing Occupations (GM) ____General Metals
    (FO)____Filing, Office Machines, Gen. Off. (VT) ____Voc.-Tech. Metals
    (SS)____Stenographic,Secretarial,Related   (BA) ____Beg. Auto
    (TO)____Typing & Related Occupations       (AA) ____Adv. Auto
                         III  Home Economics
                         _____
                         (CD) ____Child Development
                         (SO) ____S.O.S/$ Sen.
                         (H1) ____Hm. Ec. I
                         (H2) ____Hm. Ec. II
                         (AH) ____Adv. Hm. Ec.
```

Example 11B

To: Mr. John Sears   Mr. Peter Sherwood
           Mr. Jack Evans   Mr. Pat Gena

From: Mr. Bob Harris

We have had discussions with several administrators of the
Martinez Unified School District during the past year concerning
projects to be implemented on the microcomputer; for example,

>   Mike Lena   Audio-Visual Inventory
>   Laura Foster   Elementary school testing
>   Mary Aspen   High school proficiency tests
>   Rich Laughlin   Elementary school attendance
>   Bill Smith   Word processing
>   Jack Evans   Title I Management

Some of these projects are well underway; others are still in the
discussion stage.

The implementation of these requests has relied heavily on the
use of the ROP equipment, some of which is available for
administrative use approximately two hours each day.

Planning for these and future projects should be given careful
consideration by the administration. The main points to consider
are:

Hardware

We have at the high school now, or on order, the hardware to
implement these tasks at least at a minimal level.

The correcting of the elementary school tests with the inclusion
of data on each student and the Title I Management program will
probably exceed the capacity of our 5-1/4 inch disks; therefore,
consideration should be given to the purchase of a hard disk
(approximately $5,000).

Some of the projects (e.g., elementary school attendance, Title I
Management) would be more efficiently printed on a high-speed
printer (approximately $2,000).

When all of the above projects are on line along with others we
have been using for some time, we will need full-time use of at
least two terminals to obtain the output in a reasonable amount
of time. (The cost of an additional terminal will be between
$1,500 and $3,500, depending on some software information that
should be available before the end of the school year.)

(continued)

Example 11B (*continued*)

<u>Software</u>

There is also a variety of software required for the most efficient implementation of these projects.

The software should be compatible, not only for these projects, but also for those planned in the foreseeable future (two or three years). It would also be cost effective to use the same software in the high school programming and business classes and for administrative word processing.

<u>Facilities</u>

Careful consideration should be given to housing the equipment required to perform these tasks. Because of the expense required for wiring and security, their location is not easily changed.

Since this cost can be considerable, the requirements to house this equipment, provide adequate, secure storage, and provide ample space for personnel in the foreseeable future should be taken into account.

Planning is also important for the optimum utilization of the equipment. It is important that some equipment not be placed where it can be used only a small portion of the day while other equipment is overtaxed.

Easy access by the departments that make the most use of these facilities should be taken into account when locating this equipment.

<u>Cost</u>

The cost is, of course, an important factor. The district now spends in excess of $20,000 annually for computer-related services. (It may be considerably more than this; Mr. Lena would have to determine the exact amount.)

The district has potential savings from at least three sources:

(1) Direct savings by having some currently outside services performed on district computers.

(2) Indirect savings by using programs such as the inventory program, which allows better control over the audio-visual equipment and so saves some of the $6,000 in annual losses.

(3) Indirect savings by increasing efficiency with computer programs and word processing. When some personnel leave, they would not have to be replaced.

(continued)

Example 11 B (*continued*)

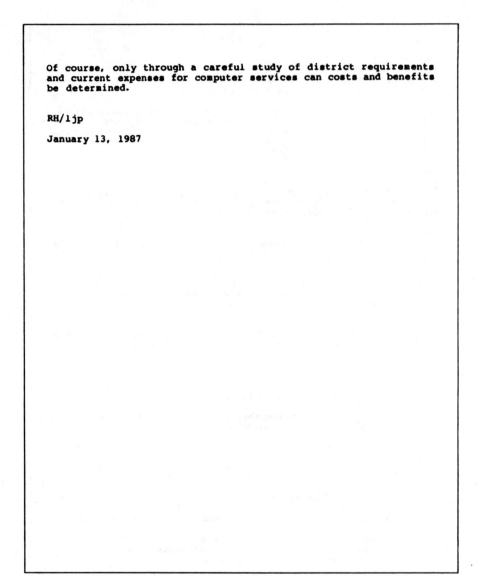

Of course, only through a careful study of district requirements
and current expenses for computer services can costs and benefits
be determined.

RH/ljp

January 13, 1987

12

PAGE AND PAGE NUMBER COMMANDS PRINTER CONTROL COMMANDS

The commands in this lesson are divided into two groups: paging commands that control page numbering and page breaks and printer control commands that handle special print functions and screen comments. Use the following chart for reference.

Paging Commands

Command	Function
.OP	Omits page numbers
.PG	Turns on page numbers
.PN	Controls page numbers
.PC	Controls page number column position (28 default)
	.PC0 center on ruler line
.PA	Inserts new page

Command	Function
.CP	Inserts conditional page
^QI	Specifies a page to go to
.UJ	Controls microjustification
.OJ	Controls on-screen justification

Printer-Control commands

Command	Function
.BP	Controls bidirectional printing
.PS	Controls proportional spacing
.SR	Controls superscript/subscript roll
.LQ	Controls letter quality printing
.BN	Controls bin number selection
.IG	Allows comments (inserted on screen but not printed)

Here again the usefulness of many of these commands depends large-ly on the type of printer you are using. Consult your printer manual and try these commands to see if they work with your printer.

OMIT PAGE NUMBERS (.OP)

You have probably noticed that for all files you have printed so far, WordStar automatically printed the page number. Entering the dot command .OP at the beginning of the page where you want page numbering turned off suppresses page numbering.

Note: Even though page numbers are not printed, they are still maintained by WordStar and you can still request to have a particular page printed.

PAGE NUMBERS ON (.PG)

Page numbering is on by default. If .OP has been entered to turn page numbering off, place .PG in the top line of the page where you want to turn page numbering back on.

PAGE NUMBER (.PN)

The .PN command allows you to set the first page number to be printed. WordStar automatically increments page numbering from this entry. If you wish to start printing page numbers on some page other than the first, type **.OP** on the first page and, at the top of the page where you wish numbering to start, type **.PN** and the first page number you want to appear. You can also use this command with documents contained in two or more files. For example, suppose that file A has 10 pages and file B, a continuation of A, has 7. At the beginning of file B, type **.PN 11**. Numbering will then begin at 11, and pages will be numbered sequentially through page 17.

PAGE NUMBER COLUMN (.PC)

 Page numbers are normally centered at the bottom of the page. The .PC command lets you control the column in which the page number is printed. Type **.PC** and the column number in which you want the page number to appear. You may also indicate in inches the distance the page number should be printed from the left margin. Follow the value with the inch symbol, ″, just as you did with the previous dot commands where inches were also used. Remember that the # character, described in the previous lesson, can be used in either the header or footer commands to indicate page number placement.

A variation of this dot command with WordStar 5 is .PC0. Following PC with a zero causes the page number to print in the center of the ruler line that is in effect when the page number is printed.

NEW PAGE (.PA)

You have no doubt noticed that when your file has reached a certain length, you get a series of dashes across the screen with a *P* in column 80. The *P* is a flag character indicating where a page break will occur when you print your file. Page breaks do not always occur where you want them, however. In long documents or documents with many charts or tables, for example, you almost always have to reposition page breaks to more appropriate places. The .PA command allows you to force a page break at whatever line you select. To know where you need to force a page break, you can type in your entire document and then return to the beginning and scroll through the document, entering the **.PA** wherever you want a new page to begin. Never work from the end of the file to the beginning, or you may end up with a first page that is only a few lines long. Remember, too, that you can add one to six lines of text to a page by changing the bottom margin.

CONDITIONAL PAGE (.CP)

A better way to avoid unwanted page breaks, but one that takes a little getting used to, is to use the .CP*n* command, where *n* is the number of lines you specify to remain on the page. This allows you to avoid having charts, tables, and so on printed over two pages. For example, if a table requires six lines, place **.CP 6** immediately above the graph. If there are not six lines remaining on the page, printing will start on the next page. On the screen, the page break, if displayed, appears as it does when the .PA command is specified.

GO TO PAGE (^QI n,+,−)

In previous lessons you worked with commands that allow you to move long distances through a file. One of the most useful commands for long documents is ^QI *n*, which sends the cursor directly to the page specified by the number *n*. If the page requested follows the cursor position, the cursor stops at the beginning of the requested page. A request to move to a page past the last numbered page will place the cursor at the end of the file. If the page requested is before the cursor position, the cursor stops at the end of the page. If page numbering has been altered by a .PN command, a request to move to a page before numbering begins will move the cursor to the beginning of the file. By specifying a +n or −n, the cursor moves forward or backward the number of pages represented by *n*.

MICROJUSTIFICATION ON/OFF/DIS (.UJ)

If your printer supports microjustification, you can use the .UJ command to set microjustification to ON, OFF, or DIS. The default value is DIS (discretionary); that is, the printer driver decides when to use microjustification. With microjustification on, spacing between words, and with some printers, between letters, is adjusted in small increments. This slows printing to some extent. If speed is of primary importance, turn microjustification off (enter **.UJ OFF**); if appearance is the main consideration, turn it on (enter **.UJ ON**). The default value DIS is usually best for most printers that support this function. However, if you find that table columns are not aligned when printed, turn microjustification off before printing tables and on again immediately after printing tables.

TURNING JUSTIFICATION ON/OFF (.OJ)

If you like, you can leave a portion of your document ragged right. Bracket that portion with .OJ ON and .OJ OFF. As usual with Word-Star, what you see on the screen is what will be printed. This feature is useful when you reformat an entire document with a section not justified. You can also use the on-screen command ^OJ to turn justification on or off.

BIDIRECTIONAL PRINT (.BP)

The .BP command allows you to turn bidirectional printing on or off. Entering **.BP 0** turns bidirectional printing off and causes printing to proceed from left to right only. Entering **.BP 1** turns bidirectional printing back on. If your printer does not use bidirectional printing, it will not be affected by this command.

PROPORTIONAL SPACING ON/OFF (.PS)

The .PS command prints the section of your document bracketed by .PS ON and .PS OFF in proportional spacing. Proportional spacing uses different amounts of space for different letters. For example, the letter *w* requires more space than the letter *a*. Wordstar maintains a table of spaces required for different letters for printers that support this feature. For this feature to work with daisy-wheel and thimble printers, the appropriate wheel or thimble must be installed. You must also select this function to properly access and control fonts on laser printers.

SUBSCRIPT/SUPERSCRIPT ROLL (.SR)

The .SR command controls how far above or below the text line subscripts and superscripts are printed. The default value for superscript and subscript roll is 3 (3/48 of an inch). To change this value, enter **.SR** followed by the number, representing a number of 48ths of an inch, that you wish subscripts or superscripts to roll up or down.

LETTER QUALITY ON/OFF/DIS(.LQ)

The .LQ command allows you to change printing quality from draft to letter quality. You can set this command at the beginning of your document or within the document to print a section. You can enter either **.LN OFF** or **.LQ0** to turn letter-quality printing off and either **.LQ ON** or **.LQ1** to turn it back on.

The option, DIS, stands for discretionary. WordStar will select letter quality ON or OFF depending on the font used.

SELECTING SHEET FEEDERS (.BN)

The .BN command allows you to select one of four sheet bins for your document. This allows you to feed into your printer letterhead plain paper, envelopes, and other types of paper held in different paper bins, if your printer accommodates such a feature. The command to enter is **.BN***n* where *n* is a number from 1 to 4 assigned by you or your printer to particular paper bins.

IGNORE (.IG, ..)

Two commands, .IG (for ignore) or dot,dot (..), allow you to insert remarks in your file that you can read on the screen, but that are not printed. Enter the command and then your comments. Note that your comments must be confined to the line with the dot command on it.

EXERCISES

1. Load Example.1.
   a. Print the example without a page number.
   b. Print the page number in the header instead of the footer.

2. Using Example.1, practice changing the page number column in both the header and footer.

3. Enter and then print Example 12A. Note the use of character-width commands. Example 12B shows the final appearance of the form.

4. Change the size of the printout by modifying the .CW and .LH commands.

5. Try any of the special print commands introduced in this lesson that apply to your printer.

Example 12A

```
.CW 7
.LH 4
.CW 10
```

	12:00	12:30	1:00	1:30	2:00	2:30	3:00	3:30	4:00	4:30	5:00	5:30	6:00	6:30	7:00
8:00	4.0	4.5	5.0	5.5	6.0	6.5	7.0	7.5	8.0	8.5	9.0	9.5			
8:30	3.5	4.0	4.5	5.0	5.5	6.0	6.5	7.0	7.5	8.0	8.5	9.0	9.5		
9:00	3.0	3.5	4.0	4.5	5.0	5.5	6.0	6.5	7.0	7.5	8.0	8.5	9.0	9.5	
9:30	2.5	3.0	3.5	4.0	4.5	5.0	5.5	6.0	6.5	7.0	7.5	8.0	8.5	9.0	9.5
10:00	2.0	2.5	3.0	3.5	4.0	4.5	5.0	5.5	6.0	6.5	7.0	7.5	8.0	8.5	9.0
10:30	1.5	2.0	2.5	3.0	3.5	4.0	4.5	5.0	5.5	6.0	6.5	7.0	7.5	8.0	8.5
11:00	1.0	1.5	2.0	2.5	3.0	3.5	4.0	4.5	5.0	5.5	6.0	6.5	7.0	7.5	8.0
11:30	0.5	1.0	1.5	2.0	2.5	3.0	3.5	4.0	4.5	5.0	5.5	6.0	6.5	7.0	7.5
12:00		0.5	1.0	1.5	2.0	2.5	3.0	3.5	4.0	4.5	5.0	5.5	6.0	6.5	7.0
12:30			0.5	1.0	1.5	2.0	2.5	3.0	3.5	4.0	4.5	5.0	5.5	6.0	6.5
1:00				0.5	1.0	1.5	2.0	2.5	3.0	3.5	4.0	4.5	5.0	5.5	6.0
1:30					0.5	1.0	1.5	2.0	2.5	3.0	3.5	4.0	4.5	5.0	5.5
2:00						0.5	1.0	1.5	2.0	2.5	3.0	3.5	4.0	4.5	5.0
2:30							0.5	1.0	1.5	2.0	2.5	3.0	3.5	4.0	4.5
3:00								0.5	1.0	1.5	2.0	2.5	3.0	3.5	4.0

Example 12B

	12:00	12:30	1:00	1:30	2:00	2:30	3:00	3:30	4:00	4:30	5:00	5:30	6:00	6:30	7:00
8:00	4.0	4.5	5.0	5.5	6.0	6.5	7.0	7.5	8.0	8.5	9.0	9.5	—	—	—
8:30	3.5	4.0	4.5	5.0	5.5	6.0	6.5	7.0	7.5	8.0	8.5	9.0	—	—	—
9:00	3.0	3.5	4.0	4.5	5.0	5.5	6.0	6.5	7.0	7.5	8.0	8.5	9.0	—	—
9:30	2.5	3.0	3.5	4.0	4.5	5.0	5.5	6.0	6.5	7.0	7.5	8.0	8.5	9.0	—
10:00	2.0	2.5	3.0	3.5	4.0	4.5	5.0	5.5	6.0	6.5	7.0	7.5	8.0	8.5	9.0
10:30	1.5	2.0	2.5	3.0	3.5	4.0	4.5	5.0	5.5	6.0	6.5	7.0	7.5	8.0	8.5
11:00	1.0	1.5	2.0	2.5	3.0	3.5	4.0	4.5	5.0	5.5	6.0	6.5	7.0	7.5	8.0
11:30	0.5	1.0	1.5	2.0	2.5	3.0	3.5	4.0	4.5	5.0	5.5	6.0	6.5	7.0	7.5
12:00	—	0.5	1.0	1.5	2.0	2.5	3.0	3.5	4.0	4.5	5.0	5.5	6.0	6.5	7.0
12:30	—	—	0.5	1.0	1.5	2.0	2.5	3.0	3.5	4.0	4.5	5.0	5.5	6.0	6.5
1:00	—	—	—	0.5	0.1	1.5	2.0	2.5	3.0	3.5	4.0	4.5	5.0	5.5	6.0
1:30	—	—	—	—	0.5	1.0	1.5	2.0	2.5	3.0	3.5	4.0	4.5	5.0	5.5
2:00	—	—	—	—	—	0.5	1.0	1.5	2.0	2.5	3.0	3.5	4.0	4.5	5.0
2:30	—	—	—	—	—	—	0.5	1.0	1.5	2.0	2.5	3.0	3.5	4.0	4.5
3:00	—	—	—	—	—	—	—	0.5	1.0	1.5	2.0	2.5	3.0	3.5	4.0

13

FIND AND
FIND AND REPLACE
COMMANDS

One of the most powerful features of any word processing system is the ability to find a given word or phrase in a file and automatically replace it with another word or phrase of your choice. WordStar provides two commands for these operations: Find and Find and Replace.

FIND (^QF)

To see how the Find command works, load Example 11B and place the cursor at the beginning of the file. To initiate the Find command select ^QF and the FIND dialog box shown below is displayed.

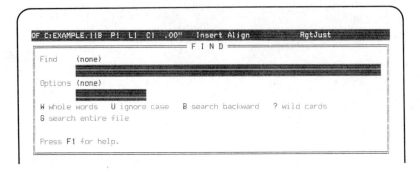

Your response in the Find field can be any group of characters (or string), partial word, word, or phrase up to 65 characters in length. For this exercise, type the word **Facilities** which occurs midway in the letter.

Press ENTER. For now, press ENTER again to bypass the Options field (Options will be dioscussed shortly). Starting from the cursor position, WordStar searches through the file for the first occurrence of the word *Facilities*. If it finds this word, it will stop at its location. If it does not find the word *Facilities* by the time it reaches the end of the file, it will display "Could not find: Facilities" and ask you to press ESC to continue. After you press ESC, the cursor will be at the end of the file. You can return to where you started and search for another string or resume editing.

RETURN TO PREVIOUS POSITION (^QP)

To return the cursor to the place in the file where it was when the last command was given, enter the command ^QP. If the Find command (^QF) was the last command entered, you will be returned to the position where that command was given.

FIND OPTIONS (W, U, B, ?, G)

At the bottom of the Find window are a set of Find options. If you just press ENTER, selecting no options, WordStar will begin its search from the cursor position, searching for an exact match to the string (word or phrase) you entered.

The following options apply to both the Find command (^QF) and the Find and Replace command (^QA, discussed next). To select an option, enter one or more of the letters displayed. More than one option can be selected at a time; just enter the letters one after another, with no spaces or punctuation marks between them, before pressing ENTER.

Option	Function
W	Finds whole words only. Therefore, *ace* will not match *race*.
U	Ignores the difference between upper- and lower-case letters. For example, *CASE* matches *case* or *Case*.
B	Searches backward from cursor position.
?	Considers ? in the search string a wild card. The ? must also be entered on the Options line. If the ? is entered in the Find string and *not* entered on the Options line, then WordStar searches for the ? character. For example, if you enter **Find:All?n**, WordStar will find the name *Allen* or *Allan* only if the ? is *also* placed on the options line.
G	Tells WordStar to begin its search at the beginning of the file.
number	Searches for the *n*th example of the Find string. For example, if *n* is 4, WordStar will find the fourth occurrence of the word you are looking for. The "Not found" message will appear if the

Option   Function

file contains the Find string less than *n* times. Note that the *number* option does not appear on the menu, but is fully functional, as you shall see.

FIND MULTIPLE OCCURRENCES OF STRING (^L)

The following example shows how to search for a word that occurs several times in the file. Select ^QF and in response to "Find what?" type **cost** and press ENTER. In response to "Option(s)?" enter **G** (start at beginning of file), **U** (ignore case), and **W** (whole words only). Your screen displays

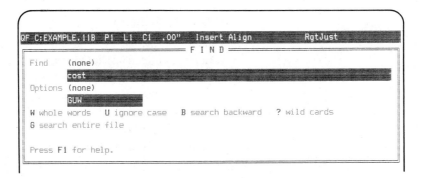

Your option selections can be entered in upper- or lowercase.

WordStar returns to the beginning of the file and starts looking for the word *cost* and stops when it finds the string of characters you requested. To have WordStar find the next occurrence of the word *cost*, type ^L; again the cursor stops after the word. Each time the cursor stops, you may delete the word, add a word, or do whatever editing you wish, and then type ^L to continue the search for the word. Note that because you specified W for whole words only on the option line, the word *costs* in the last paragraph is bypassed in the search.

This example of the Find command uses the "n" option to find the third occurrence after the cursor position of the word *cost*. Again using Example 11B enter the information so your screen matches this illustration.

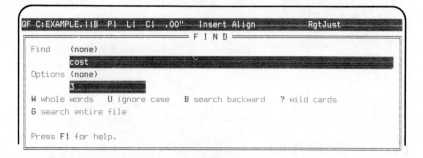

FIND AND REPLACE (^QA)

Return to the beginning of the file. You will now use the Find command with a replace operation. Select ^QA. In the Find field type **cost** and press ENTER. In the Replace field type **expense** and press ENTER. Press ENTER again in response to "Option(s)?" Before the search begins, your screen displays

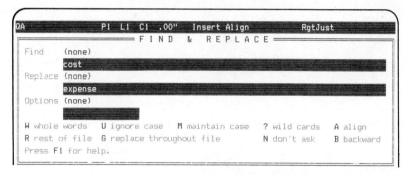

The cursor advances to the first occurrence of *cost*. In the status line is the question "Replace Y/N?" Type **Y**, and *cost* is replaced with *expense*.

Type **^L**, and the cursor advances to the next occurrence of *cost*, and the question is repeated. You can move through a file of any length in this manner, replacing or not by responding Y or N to the question.

FIND AND REPLACE OPTIONS
(W, U, M, ?, A, G, N, R, B)

Most of the options that apply to the Find command also apply directly to Find and Replace. Some, however, have modifications, and there are some additional options. The options listed here are available for Find and Replace operations in addition to those available for Find operations. The option *number* has added meaning with Find and Replace.

number	Performs a Find and Replace operation *n* times, where *n* is an integer. For example, if *n* is 4, this option tells WordStar to find and replace the next four occurrences of the word with your substitution. The "Not found" message is displayed if the command cannot be performed *n* times; however, as many Find and Replace operations as are possible will be done.
A	In most cases the replacement string is not the same length as the Find string. The A option aligns paragraphs after replacement of the Find string. After a paragraph is aligned, the cursor returns to the replaced string unless the G or R options are used, in which case the cursor will finish at the beginning or end of the file. WordStar does not hyphenate words during Find and Replace operations, even if hyphen help is on.
N	Replaces the word sought without prompting for confirmation. This feature is convenient to use with G or R so long as you are sure all occurrences of the Find string should be replaced.
R	Starts its search from the position of the cursor and searches to the end of the file.

For a time-saving application of the Find and Replace command (^QA), consider the following. Suppose you are writing a letter or report that repeats the same phrase or long word several times. Each time that word or phrase should be entered in the document, enter instead a single, uncommon character such as the ampersand (&). When you have finished the document, issue the Find and Replace command, ^QA. In response to the question "Find?" enter &. In response to "Replace?" enter your word or phrase, and in response to "Option(s)?" enter **BGNA**. WordStar will then search backward through the entire file, automatically replacing all & signs with your answer in the Replace field. Paragraphs will automatically be reformed after each replacement.

The Find and Replace command will find multiple-word strings, even if soft spaces have been inserted between the words. Also, if the word or phrase is split on two lines, it will be found, and if the word is the first or last word in the file, it will be found.

Now let's look at two examples that use the Find and Replace commands. In the first, shown here

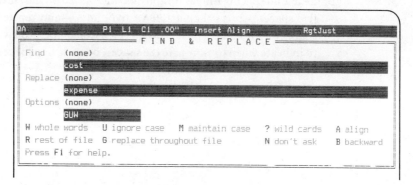

the option G causes the search to be global (through the whole file), U causes the search to ignore the distinction between upper- and lowercase letters, and W causes the search to find complete words only. Given this command, WordStar will find *Cost,* but not *costs.*

In addition to searching for words or phrases, you can also search for special formats and characters such as boldfacing, underlining, and carriage returns and replace them with other formats or special characters or eliminate them by replacing them with nothing. In this example note that when you enter ^P^S (the CTRL must be pressed with both P and S) in response to "Find?" only ^S is displayed. Similarly, in response to "Replace?" only ^B is displayed, even though you entered ^P^B.

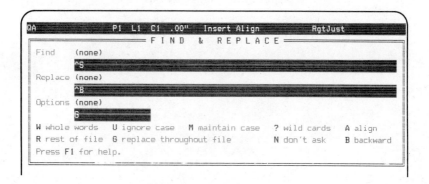

EXERCISES

1. Enter Example 13. Using the Find and Replace command, replace each occurrence of *John Philip Smith* with *Sara Lee Brown.*

2. Find every occurrence of *his* and change each to *her* if appropriate.

3. Delete all spacing for paragraph indentation. To do this, search for five spaces — press the SPACEBAR five times — and replace these spaces with no spaces (just press ENTER). Remember, you will have to indicate when to eliminate the spaces, because five spaces occur in other parts of the document.

Example 13

LAST WILL AND TESTAMENT

OF

JOHN PHILIP SMITH

I, JOHN PHILIP SMITH, presently residing in the City of
Walnut Creek, Contra Costa County, California, being of sound
and disposing mind and memory, and not acting under duress,
menace, or undue influence of any kind or person whatsoever, do
hereby make, publish and declare this to be my Last Will and
Testament in the following manner:

ARTICLE I

I hereby revoke any and all former and other Wills and
Codicils made at any time heretofore by me.

ARTICLE II

It is my intent hereby to dispose of all my property,
whether real or personal, tangible or intangible, community or
separate, wheresoever situated, that I have the right to dispose
of by Will, including all property in which I shall hereafter
acquire any interest, and further including any and all property
as to which I may hereafter acquire a power of appointment by
Will.

(continued)

Example 13 (*Continued*)

ARTICLE III

I hereby declare that I am not married. I have no children.
I have no former marriages or issue of such.

ARTICLE IV

I hereby give, devise, and bequeath one-half (1/2) of the
residue of my estate, real, personal, or mixed, of whatever kind
and wheresoever situated, equally to my parents, JOHN SMITH and
ANGELA SMITH, of Lovely Lane, Martinez Ca. 94553. If one parent
shall predecease me, then the surviving parent shall take all,
and then to their issue by right of representation.

ARTICLE V

I give, devise and bequeath one-half (1/2) of the residue of
my estate, real, personal, or mixed, of whatever kind and
wheresoever situated to my very good friend, MARCY SIMMONS, and
then to her issue by right of representation. If MARCY SIMMONS
shall predecease me, this gift shall lapse.

ARTICLE VI

I direct that all my debts, including funeral expenses,
expenses of last illness, administration expenses, and all
inheritance, estate, and other death taxes, and payment of a
family allowance, if needed, be paid by the Executrix out of the
residue of my estate from the first moneys coming into her hands
and available therefor, and shall not be charged or collected
from any beneficiary of my probate estate.

(continued)

Example 13 (*Continued*)

ARTICLE VII

I hereby nominate and request the court to appoint my friend, MARCY SIMMONS, as Executrix of this Will, to serve without bond.   Should MARCY SIMMONS serve as Executrix, I authorize her to sell, lease, convey, transfer, encumber, hypothecate, or otherwise deal with the whole or any portion of my estate, either by public or private sale, with or without notice, and without securing any prior order of the court therefor.

I further authorize my Executrix either to continue the operation of any business belonging to my estate for such time and in such manner as she may deem advisable, and for the best interests of my estate, or to sell or liquidate the business at such time and on such terms as she may deem advisable, and for the best interests of my estate.   Any operation, sale or liquidation made in good faith shall be at the risk of my estate, without liability for any resulting losses against the Executrix.

ARTICLE VIII

If any beneficiary under this Will, in any manner, directly or indirectly, contests, objects or attacks this Will or any of its provisions, any share or interest in my estate given to that contesting or objecting beneficiary under this Will is revoked and shall be disposed of in the same manner as if that beneficiary had predeceased me without issue.

(continued)

xample 13 (*Continued*)

ARTICLE IX

I have intentionally and purposely omitted and made no provision in this Will for any person not mentioned herein, whether an heir of mine or one claiming to be an heir of mine or not; and if any person, whether or not mentioned in this Will should object, contest or attack this Will or any provision hereof, I give to such person, or to each of such persons, if more than one be so contesting or objecting, the sum of Ten Dollars ($10.00), and no more, in lieu of the provisions which I might have made for such person or persons so contesting, objecting or attacking this Will.

IN WITNESS WHEREOF, I subscribe my name to this, my Last Will and Testament, this _____ day of _____, 19____, at _____, Contra Costa County, California.

_____
JOHN PHILIP SMITH

(*continued*)

Example 13 (*Continued*)

The foregoing instrument, consisting of four (4) pages and
this fifth (5th) witness page, was, at this date, by the said
JOHN PHILIP SMITH signed and published as and declared to be his
Last Will and Testament in the presence of us, who, at his
request, and in his presence, and in the presence of each other,
have signed our names as witnesses hereto.

_____residing at_____

                                    _____

_____residing at_____

                                    _____

CHARTS AND LINE DRAWING

WordStar allows you to incorporate graphic symbols in your file. How you take advantage of this capability depends on the type of work you do and the type of printer you use. The illustrations in this lesson were produced with a dot-matrix printer (the NEC P9).

ASCII AND EXTENDED CHARACTER SETS

All computers and office software packages, word processors, spreadsheets, data bases, and so on, give you access to 128 characters. These include upper- and lowercase letters, numbers, and punctuation marks. This is the ASCII (American Standard Computer Information Interchange) character set. These characters are standard screen displays for all microcomputers. Some software packages access another 128 characters, referred to as the *extended character set*. WordStar gives you access to both sets of characters.

Both sets, ASCII and extended, are listed in Appendix B. Take a look at Appendix B. The extended character set encompasses the characters numbered from 128 to 255. As you can see, a variety of characters are included—math and graphic symbols, Greek letters, and most of the letters with diacritical and accent marks used in many European languages. Note, also, that each character is associated with a number. In this lesson we will be concerned primarily with those codes that are useful with graphics, but the same procedure is used to access any of these 128 characters.

GRAPHICS CHARACTERS

WordStar makes ten of the graphics characters available with the function keys. When a function key is pressed in conjunction with the ALT key, a graphic symbol is displayed. Try this now by pressing ALT and F1 simultaneously; a vertical line is displayed *after* you release the keys. Press the space bar. Continue this process, pressing the ALT key with each of the function keys. Separate the graphics characters with a space so they don't run together. If you pressed the function keys in sequence, your screen will be similar to the one shown here.

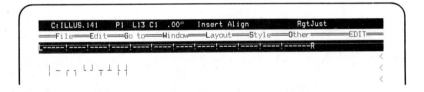

Examine the following chart that shows the graphics symbols produced when the ALT key is pressed in conjunction with a function key.

	F1	F2	F3	F4	F5	F6	F7	F8	F9	F1O
ALT	│	─	┌	┐	└	┘	┬	┴	├	┤

The chart itself was created with WordStar using all of the graphics symbols from the first illustration, plus one additional graphics symbol, the $+$. This symbol resembles a plus sign (+) but is actually extended character code 197. Look at the extended character set in Appendix B. Compare the plus sign represented by ASCII code 43 and the symbol $+$ represented by code 197.

To display the $+$ symbol on the screen, hold down the ALT key and, *using the key pad,* enter **197**. Release the ALT key, and the symbol is displayed. Two points to keep in mind: (1) You cannot use the numbers across the top of the keyboard for this operation, and (2) when using the keypad you do not have to press NUMLOCK (it doesn't matter whether it is pressed or not).

The following illustration shows a portion of the graphics symbols used to create the chart in the preceding illustration with some blank rows and columns inserted. Now you can see the individual graphics symbols used in its construction.

Construct a graphics function-key chart, like the one just shown, using the ALT function key combination. Where you see the $+$ symbol, enter ALT-197. If you frequently use this symbol or any member of the extended character set, you can define a use with the Shorthand menu to create a macro to produce the symbol. For example, entering **X** as the character to be defined and pressing ALT-197 (be sure to hold down ALT as you enter the numbers) in the definition line of the Shorthand menu allows you to display the symbol $+$ by pressing ESC-X.

THE EXTENDED CHARACTER MENU

Another method of selecting a member of the Extended character set is from the EXTENDED CHARACTER MENU. Select $^\wedge$**P0** and your screen displays:

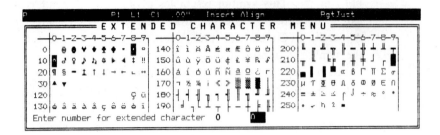

This menu shows all of the extended character set plus the Special character set that have the ASCII values from 0 to 31 (0 prints a blank).

Notice at the bottom of this dialog box you can enter the number for the character you wish to print. For example, to print the mathematic symbol for pi, π, you would enter 227 and press ENTER. Pi is printed at the position of the cursor. When working with this dialog box either set of number keys may be used to enter the number for the symbol. The special symbols are discussed in the last section of this lesson.

PRODUCING GRAPHS

Symbols 176-178 and 219-223 lend themselves very nicely to graphs, as shown in the following illustration.

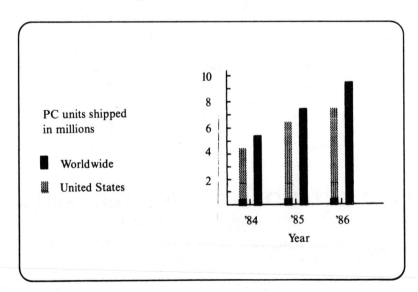

The x and y axes were produced using the built-in graphics character codes. The vertical bars were made using codes 178 and 219 with a little help from code 222 to fill in the bottom of the lighter bars.

If you do a lot of this type of work, you might consider creating the x and y axes and then saving them in a file so you can read them into a file whenever you need them. You can further simplify your work if, when you complete one set of bars, you use the Block Copy command (column mode) to place them in subsequent positions. You can then add or delete individual symbols to obtain the right height. You also use the Shorthand menu to create a macro that inserts multiple symbols at one time.

As a final example of the usefulness of graphics symbols, let's place a box around some text, as shown here.

```
It's not a bug,
it's an undocumented feature
```

You can facilitate your use of boxes by creating a box large enough to contain the contents of a standard page and storing it in a disk file. When you want to box material (be sure to type the material first, before attempting to box it), you can read the box into the current file (by pressing ^KR) and cut it down to the desired size with appropriate Block and Column Delete operations. Then, using the Column Replace command (^KN followed by ^KI), you can block off the material and place it in the box. What would happen if you blocked off the box and tried to place it around the material? Try it if you're not sure. Remember the Undo command.

SPECIAL CHARACTERS

With WordStar 5 the special symbols represented by the ASCII values 0 through 31 can now be displayed. Again, you can examine these symbols in Appendix B. To display the values on the screen, use the same procedure you did to display those with ASCII values greater than 127; press ALT and a *keypad* number from 0 to 31. When ALT is released the symbol is displayed. The ability to print these symbols, of course, depends on your printer.

EXERCISES

1. Using the Shorthand menu, create a set of macros that will produce the graphics symbols used to form the box in the last illustration of this lesson. Using the ESC key, enter the numbers in sequence, from 0-9, to produce the symbols.

2. The following illustration shows all of the function key commands provided with WordStar. Create this illustration and save it on a file; then print it to use for reference. When you want to customize WordStar with the values best suited to your work and to assign function key commands most convenient to you, you can modify this chart accordingly. Customizing is performed using WSCHANGE, as discussed in Appendix D.

	F1	F2	F3	F4	F5	F6	F7	F8	F9	F10
Function	^J	^U	^PS	^PB	^Y	^T	^B	^OO	^KS	^KD
SHIFT	^OD	^OC	^QL	^QN	^KY	^KH	^KV	^KC	^KB	^KK
CTRL	^QF	^QA	^L	^QI	.LM	.RM	.PM6	.PA	^QS	^QD
ALT	│	─	┌	┐	└	┘	┬	┴	├	┤

3. Create a large rectangle with either graphics symbols provided with WordStar or those you worked with in Exercise 1. Save it in a file for later use.

15

INDEXING
TABLE OF CONTENTS
FOOTNOTES/
ENDNOTES
PARAGRAPH
NUMBERING
LINE NUMBERING

If the work you do includes producing manuals, documentation, or books, you will find the Indexing and Table of Contents commands very useful.

An index is an alphabetical list of words or topics in a document along with the page number where they may be found. Similarly, a table of contents is a sequential list of the sections in a document, also including page numbers. Because page numbers are part of both an index and a table of contents, these are the final pieces of a document you create. You must complete all formatting and editing prior to starting the index and table of contents.

TRADITIONAL METHOD OF INDEXING WITH WORDSTAR (^PK, .IX)

There are two methods of indexing a document with WordStar. One is very similar to the traditional index card method. Here is an outline of the traditional—manual—way of indexing.

1. Read your document, marking the words or phrases that you want to place in the index.

2. Read the document again, copying each word or phrase, along with the page number, on an index card.

3. Sort the cards alphabetically.

4. Consolidate the page number for identical entries on one card.

5. Type the list in proper format for your index.

With WordStar, you use the same approach. You again mark the items you want in the index, but this time you mark them electronically, using the commands ^PK, .IX, or ^ONI.

The command ^PK is used to bracket words or phrases that you want in the index. The index selection appears in reverse video and is bracketed by ^K. The ^K symbols can be removed with the print display toggle, ^OD.

If a topic you wish in the index does not appear appropriately in the text, you may enter it in one of two ways.

1. Enter the dot command **.IX** in proper position and follow it with the index entry.

2. Select "Index entry" from the Other menu or enter the command ^**ONI**. In either case you are presented with the INDEX dialog box with a field where you place your index entry.

Note: If you wish the page number for your index entry to appear in bold enter a "+" sign before the entry.

Enter **.IX** or ^**ONI** before the paragraph or section the command refers to. Avoid placing it in the middle of a paragraph; otherwise, it may get included in the paragraph during a reform paragraph operation. Now let's see how this method of indexing works.

Load a file that is edited and formatted and ready for indexing and then follow these steps (illustrations of the steps will follow shortly).

1. Bracket the word or phrase you want in the index with $^\wedge$**PK** or enter one of the commands, **.IX** or $^\wedge$**ONI** followed by a topic you want included.

2. With the document marked, save it and return to the opening menu.

You are now ready to let WordStar do the hard part: alphabetizing, collating, and placing the data in index format.

Let's try this traditional procedure now. By necessity, a long example is required to produce a useful illustration of an index (and a table of contents). For this example we will use Lesson 13 and our document file will be called L13.WS5. The following illustration shows two sections of that lesson and is very similar to what you would obtain if you marked Lesson 13 for indexing.

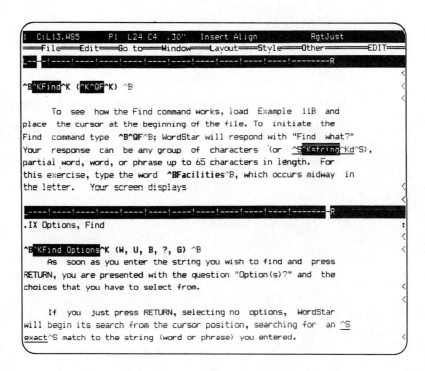

When all items are marked for the index, you are ready to index. With the marked file saved at the opening menu, display the Other menu and select **I** (index a document). The screen displays

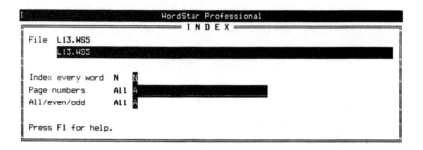

Enter the file name and press ENTER. Respond **N** to the question "Index every word (Y/N)?" The following questions allow you to select the pages you wish to index. Just as with printing, you can press ESC to select the default responses to the questions. Indexing starts immediately and takes about six seconds for a document of 2000 words on an IBM XT. On the status line the page number advances as indexing proceeds. When indexing is finished, an index file is produced with the same name as your file, but with the extension .IDX.

The index file produced for Lesson 13 is shown here:

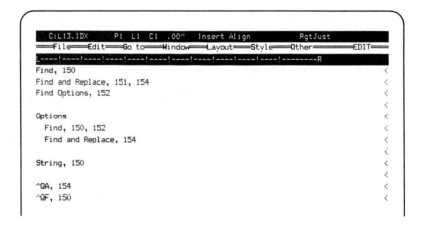

Note that the page references will be off because to create this example, an arbitrary page number, 150, was introduced with the .PN command.

An index file may be loaded into WordStar like any other document. You then have all the WordStar editing features available to you to modify it in any manner you please.

EXCLUSION METHOD OF INDEXING WITH WORDSTAR

The second method of indexing with WordStar may seem a little cumbersome at first, but once you've tried it, you will find it to be a very efficient and easy method of indexing. We will refer to it as the exclusion method because it requires two exclusion files, files that contain the words you *don't* want in the index. One file is provided by WordStar and the other is created by you (with the help of WordStar). The exclusion file provided by WordStar is named WSINDEX.XCL and should be on your disk. It is a list of words that almost never are included in an index. You can examine this file with WordStar to see the type of words it contains. You create the second exclusion file, using WordStar, as described here.

Again, your document should be in final form with formatting and editing done. The first step is to create your exclusion file.

From the Other menu select **I**. In response to the question "Index every word (Y/N)?" enter **Y**. Press ESC to give the default response to the next two questions. Indexing starts immediately; this time every word is indexed. This process takes about 10 seconds for a file of 2000 words. Again, an index file is produced with the same name as your file, but with the extension .IDX. A small section of this five-page file, again using Lesson 13, is shown here.

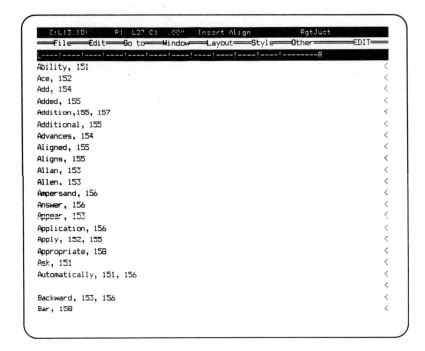

```
    C:L13.IDX        P1  L27 C1   .00"   Insert Align          RgtJust
    ══File══════Edit══════Go to══════Window══════Layout══════Style══════Other══════════════EDIT══
    L────!────!────!────!────!────!────!────!────!────!────!─────────R
    Ability, 151                                                              <
    Ace, 152                                                                  <
    Add, 154                                                                  <
    Added, 155                                                                <
    Addition,155, 157                                                         <
    Additional, 155                                                           <
    Advances, 154                                                             <
    Aligned, 155                                                              <
    Aligns, 155                                                               <
    Allan, 153                                                                <
    Allen, 153                                                                <
    Ampersand, 156                                                            <
    Answer, 156                                                               <
    Appear, 153                                                               <
    Application, 156                                                          <
    Apply, 152, 155                                                           <
    Appropriate, 158                                                          <
    Ask, 151                                                                  <
    Automatically, 151, 156                                                   <
                                                                              <
    Backward, 153, 156                                                        <
    Bar, 158                                                                  <
```

This file is the first step in producing your exclusion file. The second and last step is to scroll through this file, *deleting all the words you want in your index,* saving the file and making it an exclusion file by keeping the first name and changing the extension from .IDX to .XCL.

Now, if you go back and index the same document, again answering **Y** to the question "Index every word (Y/N)?" and pressing ESC to give the default responses to the next two questions, you will have an index of your document. All the words in WordStar's exclusion file and the exclusion file you created are omitted, leaving only those words you deleted from the previous index file.

SUBREFERENCES AND CROSS-REFERENCES

The following example shows the .IX command used in subreference format.

.IX Commands, Dot commands

When the file containing this command is indexed, the printout will look like this:

Commands

Dot commands, page number

If you want to use a topic as a cross-reference, precede it with a hyphen as in the following example.

.IX—Indexing commands. *See* Dot commands

With an entry of this type, no page number is included.

When using either $^\wedge$PK or .IX, the maximum length of the word or phrase to be indexed is 50 characters, including any subreferences.

TABLE OF CONTENTS (.TC)

The procedure for producing a table of contents is similar to the "traditional" method for producing an index. When your document is in final form, go through it entering the dot command **.TC** above the items you want in the table of contents. With the .TC command, you have to state specifically if you want page numbers included. You do this by placing a number sign (#) in the column where the numbers will be. Place the # symbol on the same line as the .TC command.

Using LESSON 13 follow these steps:

1. Enter **.RR** or **.TB** to set up a ruler line with a tab where you want the page numbers to appear (be sure at least one hyphen is after the tab).

2. Enter **.TC** above the item you want in the table of contents.

3. Place the cursor on the line containing the item to be included, delete the item, and then replace it with the Undo command, ^U.

4. Position the cursor after the .TC command and press ^U to also place the deleted item on the dot command (.TC) line.

5. Enter ^P. to enter ellipses (periods) up to the tab mark you entered in step 1.

6. Enter the symbol #.

An example of how a table of contents entry will appear, with ellipses, is shown here.

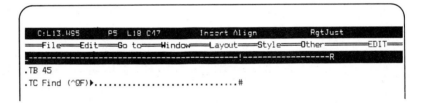

A note of caution: If you use Undo (^U) to place text after .TC or .IX, the flag will be deleted if the Undo line terminates with a soft carriage return. Move the cursor to the end of the line and press ENTER (with insert on), and the flag (:) will return in column 80.

You may use the special print commands — underline, bold, and so on — in the .TC line. Also, any spacing you enter will be retained.

You may have up to nine separate table of contents listing files for a single document. For example, you can use .TC for the table of contents, .TC1 for a list of all illustrations, .TC2 for a list of tables, and so on. The following illustration shows a portion of a file (LESSON13) with two Table of Contents commands used.

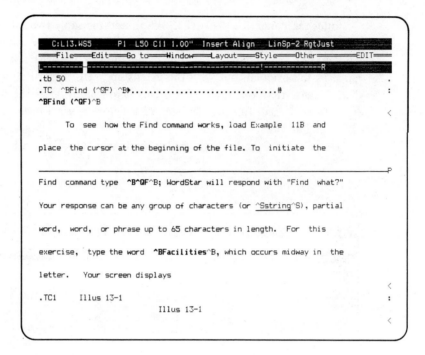

When you have finished with the .TC commands and text, save the file. Select **T** from the opening menu, and the screen displays

Enter the name of the file (L13.WS5), and the same two questions presented with indexing are displayed. Press ESC to prepare a table of contents for the complete file. On completion, a file with the same name as the original, but with the extension .TOC, is written to the disk. If more than one table of contents is produced, after the extension .TOC is used, further files are labeled in numerical order, .TO1, .TO2, and so on.

The table of contents produced from Lesson 13 is shown here.

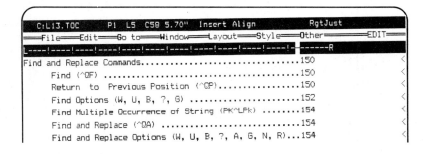

```
C:L13.TOC     P1  L5  C59 5.70"  Insert Align          RgtJust
===File====Edit====Go to====Window===Layout===Style===Other========EDIT===
L----!----!----!----!----!----!----!----!----!----!-------R
Find and Replace Commands..................................150        <
       Find (^QF) ........................................150        <
       Return to Previous Position (^QP)................150        <
       Find Options (W, U, B, ?, G) .....................152        <
       Find Multiple Occurrence of String (PK^LPk) ........154        <
       Find and Replace (^QA) ...........................154        <
       Find and Replace Options (W, U, B, ?, A, G, N, R)...154        <
```

The following sample, also from Lesson 13, shows a list of illustrations.

```
C:ILLUS.TOC    P1  L7  C1   .00"   Insert Align          RgtJust
===File====Edit====Go to====Window===Layout===Style===Other========EDIT===
L----!----!----!----!----!----!----!----!----!----!--------R
    Illus. 13-1                    150                                 <
    Illus. 13-2                    151                                 <
    Illus. 13-3                    152                                 <
    Illus. 13-4                    153                                 <
    Illus. 13-5                    153                                 <
    Illus. 13-6                    153                                 \
```

After these files are produced by WordStar, you may open them for editing as you would any other file.

FOOTNOTES AND ENDNOTES

WordStar 5 allows you to enter footnotes and endnotes. Footnotes are printed at the bottom of each page. Endnotes are printed at the end of each file or chapter. Also available to further explain items in a file are comments and annotations. Comments appear only on screen to enhance the explanation of some item. Annotations print like footnotes—at the bottom of the page.

THE NOTES MENU (^ON)

To create one of these four types of notes, press ^ON or select it from the Other menu. The Notes menu shown below is displayed.

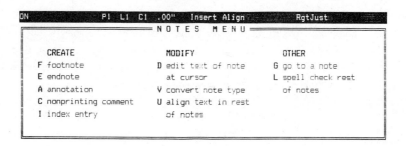

To enter one of the four types of notes, select from the menu the first letter of the note type you wish to use, **F** for footnote, **E** for endnote, **A** for annotation, or **C** for comment.

Before we go into the characteristics of these notes, let's look at the remaining items in this window.

Display Note (D)

You may display and edit any previously entered note types by placing the cursor on the desired note and selecting **D**. WordStar's full range of editing features is available to edit notes.

Changing Note Types (V)

Selecting **V** changes a note from one type to another. Place the cursor on a note before selecting **V**. A dialog box is displayed where you make your selection of the note type you wish to change to. Renumbering of the notes takes place automatically.

Align Text (U)

If you change the margins for your notes, selecting **U** will reformat your notes within those margins, starting at the note the cursor is on and proceeding through the notes to the end of the file.

Go to Note (G)

You can quickly locate a note by selecting **G**. On making this selection you are presented with a dialog box where you may select the type of note to find. When that selection is made, you are presented with the Find Note window which is similar in appearance and function to the Find window used with a standard file.

Check Note Spelling (L)

Using the standard file spelling check does not check the spelling in the various note types. To check the note spelling, select **L** from the Notes menu. The spelling is checked in each type of note from the position of the cursor to the end of the file.

NOTE CHARACTERISTICS

The general characteristics for the four type notes are as follows:

Automatic Numbering

In each file the notes are, by default, automatically numbered beginning with 1. The sequence and type of numbering may be changed.

Combine Note Types

Any combination of notes, including all four types, may be used in a single document.

Note Sequence Options

You have the option of using one of three note sequencing systems:

Numbers: 1, 2, 3 (see .f#, .e#)
Alpha: A - Z, AA - ZZ, AAA - ZZZ
Symbol: *, **, ***

Footnote Separator

A line of dashes is automatically inserted between text and footnotes on each page.

Size Limitation

There is effectively no size limit on any of the four types of notes (each note can be up to 40K or approximately fifteen pages).

Full Editing Capabilities

When in any of the note windows, you may use WordStar's full editing capabilities.

Auto Renumbering

If you add or delete notes or move a block of text in your file that contains a note, all notes are automatically "resequenced" regardless of whether they are numbered, lettered, or sequenced with symbols.

Converting Notes at Print Time

The dot command .CV may be used to convert notes from one type to another. The possibilities are

.CV f>e	print footnotes as endnotes
.CV e>f	print endnotes as footnotes
.CV c>f	print comments as footnotes
.CV c>e	print comments as endnotes

Place the command at the beginning of your file.

Placement of Endnotes

You can use the dot command .PE (print endnote) to control the print placement of endnotes. As an example, you may have more than one chapter in a file with endnotes for each chapter. By placing .PE at the end of each chapter within a file, you can have the endnotes that apply to a particular chapter print at the end of that chapter.

Customizing the Notes Format

Using WSCHANGE you can customize the format for printing notes. The primary items that may be customized are: default margins, line spacing, line height, position on page, title line, and separator line.

PARAGRAPH/LINE NUMBERING

In some types of legal documents, it is necessary to print paragraph numbers and/or line numbers.

Paragraph Numbering (^OZ)

Paragraph numbering offers a wide variety of formats. To enter a paragraph number, place the cursor where you want the number to appear and enter ^**OZ**. The dialog box below is displayed. In this case it displays the default starting value, one.

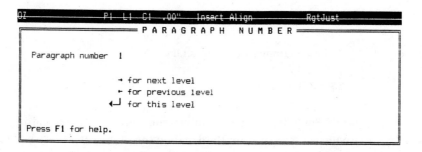

As you progress through a file numbering the paragraphs, the numbers automatically increment. The paragraph number displayed is the one that will be printed if ENTER is pressed. Press the right-arrow key to move to the next level; in this case it would be 1.1. Pressing the left-arrow moves you to the previous level (in this illustration there is no previous level).

SETTING THE PARAGRAPH NUMBER (.P#)   To start paragraph numbering at a set value, enter the dot command **.P#** and the desired value. For example, **.P# 2.7** will number the next paragraph 2.7 when ^**OZ** is selected and ENTER pressed. The value, 2.7, may be changed up or down a level using the left and right arrows.

PARAGRAPH NUMBER FORMATTING   The dot command .P# may also be used to set the paragraph number to another style or format. In addition to numbers, a letter or Roman numeral format may be used. Letters and numbers may be mixed in the same sequence. The table below shows the code and its function as it is used with the .P# command.

Code	Function
Z	uppercase letters
z	lowercase letters
I	uppercase Roman numerals
i	lowercase Roman numerals
9	numbers

As an example, the command

.P# Z.9.z

would begin the paragraph numbering with A. The second paragraph would be A.1 and the third paragraph A.1.a. If other symbols are entered in the .P# command, WordStar assumes they should be printed as entered. For example, the command **.p# [2.5]** will start the paragraph numbers with 2.5 and enclose all subsequent paragraph numbers in brackets. The paragraph symbol, ¶ , or the section symbol, §, may be entered in the .P# command by using ALT-20 or ALT-21. Check your printer manual to be sure it can print these symbols.

Line Numbering

The command used to print line numbers is the dot command .L#. Its format is

.L# style spacing, column.

STYLE   Style has two possible values:

d   Line numbers will start at 1 and be continuous from page to page.

p   Line numbers start from 1 at the beginning of each page.

SPACING   Spacing can be the values 1, 2, or 0/blank.

1   Sets single spacing.

2   Sets double spacing.

0/blank   Either entering 0 or leaving the space blank turns line numbering off.

COLUMN   Column sets the number of columns the line number will print to the *left* of the text.

The default value for column is 3. For example, if you are using the default left margin of 8, then a column value of 3 will print the numbers three columns to the *left* of the text or five columns from the paper's left edge. As an example, the command

.L# d 2,3

causes line numbers to print continuous from page to page (d), double spaced (2), and three columns to the *left* of the text (3).

EXERCISES

1. Use one of your own documents or enter Lesson 13 and use the traditional method to produce an index. If you use the .PN command to set the page number, it must be in the first line of your file.

2. Use the same document and again produce the index, this time using the exclusion method.

3. Create a table of contents and at the same time a list of tables or figures for a document you have that contains tables or figures.

4. Use one of your existing files to experiment with paragraph numbering. In addition to starting with the default value, use format codes to start the paragraph with Roman numerals and a letter/number combination.

5. Using an existing file, enter line numbers. Have the numbers begin with one on each page and the lines double spaced.

6. On one of your longer documents experiment using both endnotes and footnotes.

7. In the previous example convert all the footnotes to endnotes when the document is printed.

MISCELLANEOUS COMMANDS MENUS

The purpose of Lesson 16 is twofold. It briefly discusses the WordStar commands not previously introduced. These are commands that are not used frequently by many people, but you just may find a nugget here that will be very useful to you. The lesson also presents WordStar's traditional and pull-down menus, useful for quick reference.

Review the commands presented in this section to be aware of what they do. This way, should you ever need to perform one of the functions these commands control, you will know that WordStar has a command to help you.

REPEAT (^QQ)

The ^QQ command is used to repeat a command at a controlled rate. For instance, if you wish to scroll through a file from beginning to end in order to proofread the file, place the cursor at the beginning of the file and type $^\wedge$**QQ**$^\wedge$**Z**. The text will advance on the screen one line at a time. The speed at which the text scrolls can be increased or decreased by pressing the numbers 1 through 9: 1 is the fastest rate, 9 is the slowest rate; 3 is the default value. You can also display successive screens, either forward or backward, by typing $^\wedge$**QQ**$^\wedge$**C** or $^\wedge$**QQ**$^\wedge$**R**. Load one of your examples and try this command. Note in these commands that the CTRL key must be pressed along with each of the letters Z, C, and R. Forgetting to press CTRL would cause the letter (Z, C, or R) to be printed repeatedly in your file. (Should this happen, press the ESC key.)

CHARACTER COUNT ($^\wedge$Q?)

The command $^\wedge$Q? gives you the character or byte count from the beginning of the file up to the position of the cursor.

On the Quick Menu this command is referred to as "char count." In the window that reports the result, the reference is to byte count. Byte count is a more accurate description since included in the count are bytes that are only significant internally to WordStar and are not visible on the screen. For example, if the cursor is at the beginning of the file, selecting $^\wedge$**Q?** will give the result "Byte count at cursor: 128". With the cursor at any position in the file, you can use $^\wedge$**K?** to determine a word count and byte count for the entire file.

PHANTOM SPACE/RUBOUT ($^\wedge$PF, $^\wedge$PG)

Daisy wheel and thimble printers sometimes have special characters on their wheels or thimbles. Such characters are called by ASCII codes 32 and 127. They can be accessed with WordStar by using the commands $^\wedge$PF and $^\wedge$PG. On the screen, the symbols $^\wedge$F and $^\wedge$G will be displayed. If your printer has such characters in these positions, try this command and see what prints.

ASSIGN/CHANGE FORM FEED (^PL, .XL)

You can place a form feed in a file by pressing ^**PL**. The symbol ^L will appear at the left of the screen along with a dotted line (just as with a page break) across the page. An F will appear in the flag column. When you print the file, and the printing reaches this point, the printer will scroll to the next page and begin printing. No page number or footer will print on a page containing a ^PL command.

It may be that your printer requires a different form-feed symbol than the one provided by WordStar's printer driver. In that case you can enter the dot command .XL followed by the correct form-feed symbol for your printer. You will have to consult your printer manual to determine whether your printer supports this feature and what the proper symbol is.

RUNNING A DOS COMMAND WHILE EDITING (^KF)

In addition to being able to issue a DOS command from the opening menu, you can also issue such a command while editing. Press ^**KF** and the screen displays

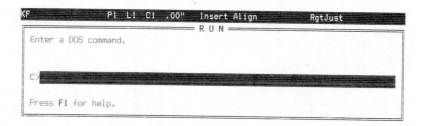

Issue the DOS command you wish. On its completion, you will be asked to press any key to return to WordStar.

DEFINING CUSTOM PRINT CONTROLS (^PQ, ^PW, ^PE, ^PR, ^P!, .XQ, .XW, .XE, .XR)

Here again are some commands that depend on the printer you use. These commands allow you access, through WordStar, to the special features of your printer such as printing double width.

There are two ways to control these custom print-control commands: using the appropriate dot commands and using WSCHANGE.

When you use dot commands to enter printer codes in your file, you must enter these codes in the form WordStar expects, which is base 16. Base 16 is the hexadecimal (hex) base. The values you need will be in your printer manual in the proper format. For example, the hex values 1B 0E turn on double-width printing for an Epson or compatible printer, and the hex value 14 will turn it off.

WordStar provides four dot commands for entering these hex codes in your files: .XQ, .XW, .XE, .XR. To implement the codes, you then use the corresponding special print codes: ^PQ, ^PW, ^PE, ^PR. For example, if the dot commands .XQ 1B OE and .XW 14 are in your file, entering **^PQYour Name^PW** (displayed as ^QYour Name^W) will print your name in double width on an Epson printer (or other printer that uses Epson printer codes). The following illustration shows the screen display.

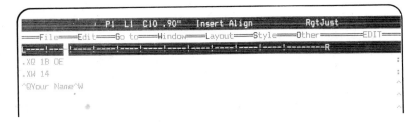

The output produced by the preceding file is as follows.

Your Name

The custom print controls are each limited to 24 bytes. The dot commands override custom print controls installed using the second method, PRCHANGE.

In addition to defining custom print controls with the dot command discussed here or using PRCHANGE, you can also use ^P! to define the custom print code at the time of entry. This procedure would normally be used only with a one-time entry. Press^P! and the dialog box shown below is displayed.

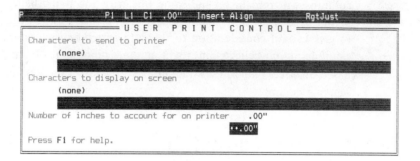

In the top field enter the special print codes to be sent to your printer. Some codes must be preceded by special symbols. They are

- The caret (^) symbol must precede a control code.
- To enter a hex value type %x before the number (to enter 1B type **%x1B**).
- To enter % type **%%**.

In the second field enter the character you wish to display on the screen to indicate custom print. This is the symbol that displays when ^OD toggles display off. (With display on, the codes entered in field 1 are displayed.)

Sorting Text (^KZ)

You can sort lines of text in a WordStar file by blocking off the text and selecting the sort command, ^**KZ**. This operation is particularly useful with a list. For example, you might have a list of family members and friends with their names, phone numbers, birthdays, ages, and addresses. Use ^**KB** and ^**KK** to block off the list and select

$^\wedge$**KZ** to sort the list. As soon as you select $^\wedge$**KZ** a message appears on the screen asking: "Sort into ascending or descending order (A/D)?". Enter your choice and the list is immediately sorted.

You can also select column mode, $^\wedge$KN, block off any column and sort the list in ascending or descending order based on the items in that column. The associated items on the same line but in other columns will remain on the same line with the items being sorted. With this idea in mind then, whenever you create a list it's worthwhile to give careful consideration to the data sorted in each column. For example, if you believe you might at some point want to sort the list based on street names, the street number and street name should be in separate columns.

Reprinting The Screen ($^\wedge$ \\)

Though very uncommon, it can sometimes happen that electrical interference or the disk operating system, DOS, can place extraneous characters on the screen. These extra characters are not in your WordStar file. To reprint your screen, press $^\wedge$ \\. The screen is reprinted with only those characters contained in the file.

WORDSTAR'S MENUS

There are two basic sets of menus with WordStar 5, traditional and pull-down. First let's consider the traditional menus.

TRADITIONAL MENUS

In addition to the opening menu, there are four editing menus ($^\wedge$O, $^\wedge$K, $^\wedge$P, and $^\wedge$Q) and six special menus (shorthand, math, print, and protected versions of $^\wedge$O, $^\wedge$K, and $^\wedge$Q) available while working with a WordStar file.

After selecting 5 to open a new File with Speed Write, your file is loaded and the Edit menu appears on the screen. It includes Cursor, Scroll, Delete, Erase, Other, and Menus options.

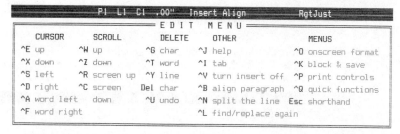

```
        P1  L1  C1  .00"   Insert Align          RgtJust
                    = E D I T   M E N U =
    CURSOR      SCROLL        DELETE    OTHER              MENUS
^E up        ^W up         ^G char    ^J help        ^O onscreen format
^X down      ^Z down       ^T word    ^I tab         ^K block & save
^S left      ^R screen up  ^Y line    ^V turn insert off  ^P print controls
^D right     ^C screen     Del char   ^B align paragraph  ^Q quick functions
^A word left    down       ^U undo    ^N split the line   Esc shorthand
^F word right                         ^L find/replace again
```

To access a menu, enter the menu prefix and the menu options will be displayed on the screen. When you have selected an option, the command will be entered in your file, and the screen will again display your text.

Block and Save Menu (^K)

This option displays commands for saving files, block operations, and file and disk operations.

```
K       P1  L1  C1  .00"   Insert Align      RgtJust
                = B L O C K   &   S A V E   M E N U =
    SAVE                BLOCK              FILE                CURSOR
D save  T save as   B begin block   C copy   O copy      0-9 set
S save & resume     K end block     V move   E rename        marker
X save & exit       H display on    Y delete J delete
Q abandon changes   W write to disk M math   P print         CASE
    WINDOW          ? word count    Z sort   L change drive/dir  " upper
A copy between      N turn column mode on  R insert a file   ' lower
G move between      I turn column replace on  F run a DOS command  . sentnce
```

Onscreen Format Menu (^O)

This option displays commands for setting margins, tabs, and toggles.

```
O       P1  L1  C1  .00"   Insert Align      RgtJust
                = O N S C R E E N   F O R M A T   M E N U =
    MARGINS & TABS          TYPING                    DISPLAY
L left    X release   W turn word wrap off   D turn print controls off
R right              J turn justification off  H turn auto-hyphenation on
T turn ruler off     E enter soft hyphen    P page preview
O ruler to text      S set line spacing     B turn soft space dots on
I set/clear tabs     C center line          K open or switch window
G temporary indent   V vertically center    M size current window
Z paragraph number   A turn auto-align off   N notes
```

Print Controls Menu (^P)

This option displays commands for special print effects.

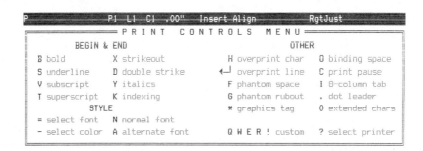

Quick Menu (^Q)

This option displays commands for cursor-movement, find, erase, spell, and scroll operations.

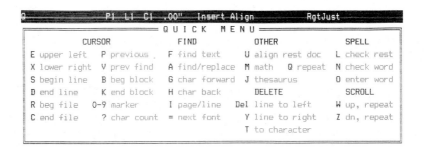

Shorthand Menu (ESC)

This option displays the macros supplied by WordStar and allows you to create your own.

```
                    P1  L1  C1  .00"  Insert Align            RgtJust  ◄
┌══════════════════════════ S H O R T H A N D   M E N U ══════════════════┐
│ ? display and/or change definitions           F1 help                   │
│                                                                          │
│ = result from last ^QM or ^KM math            @ today's date            │
│ $ formatted result from last ^QM or ^KM math  ! current time            │
│ # last ^QM math equation                                                 │
└──────────────────────────────────────────────────────────────────────────┘
  A repeat                    C Center               M Memo
  S Sincerely                 T Transpose Word
```

Math Menu (^QM)

This option displays all the math functions available to you through
calculator mode.

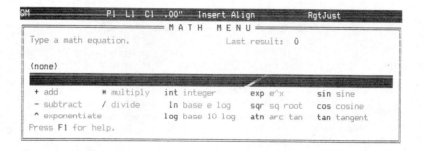

```
QM                  P1  L1  C1  .00"  Insert Align            RgtJust
┌══════════════════════════ M A T H   M E N U ═══════════════════════════┐
│ Type a math equation.              Last result:  0                       │
│                                                                          │
│ (none)                                                                   │
│ ═══════════════════════════════════                                      │
│ + add        * multiply    int integer      exp e^x      sin sine       │
│ - subtract   / divide      ln base e log     sqr sq root  cos cosine     │
│ ^ exponentiate             log base 10 log   atn arc tan  tan tangent    │
│ Press F1 for help.                                                       │
└──────────────────────────────────────────────────────────────────────────┘
```

Print File Menu (P)

This menu shows the options available when printing is interrupted. To
access this menu, press **P** when printing is in progress.

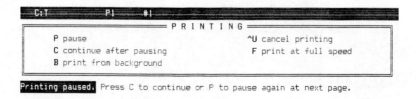

```
C:T             P1      #1
┌════════════════════════════ P R I N T I N G ════════════════════════════┐
│ P pause                            ^U cancel printing                    │
│ C continue after pausing           F print at full speed                 │
│ B print from background                                                  │
└──────────────────────────────────────────────────────────────────────────┘
Printing paused. Press C to continue or P to pause again at next page.
```

Protected Menu

When a file is protected, the menus change to reflect the restricted
number of commands available to you. Basically, you can look at a file,

but you cannot edit it. The protected versions of the Block and Save, Onscreen, and Quick menus are shown here.

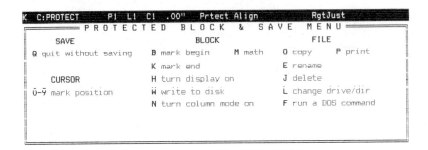

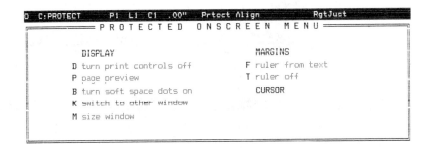

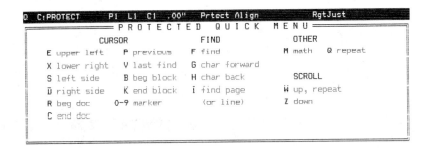

PULL-DOWN MENUS

The pull-down menus offer a selection of WordStar commands just as the traditional menus do. The basic differences are in the way the commands are organized plus the fact that you may select commands using the up and down arrows, as well as by typing the commands. Note that not all WordStar commands are available from the pull-down menus as they are from the traditional menus.

The pull-down menus are organized into more closely associated functions than are the traditional menus. The following illustrations show the command available from each pull-down menu.

File Menu

The File menu has the commands that affect the whole file such as Save, Print, Copy, and so on.

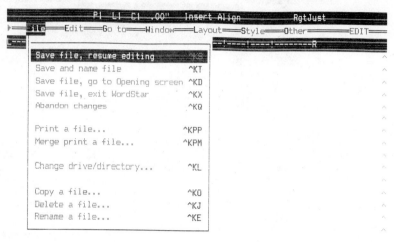

Edit Menu

The edit menu has the commonly used edit commands that deal with deleting and blocking.

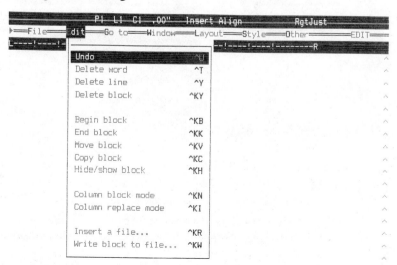

Go To Menu

The Go To menu contains the longer cursor movement commands plus the Find commands.

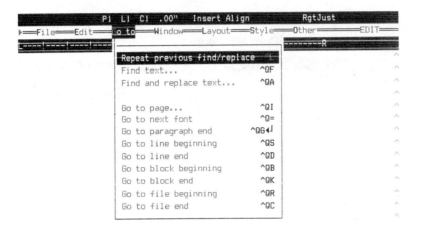

Window Menu

The window menu deals with all the commands that involve multiple windows.

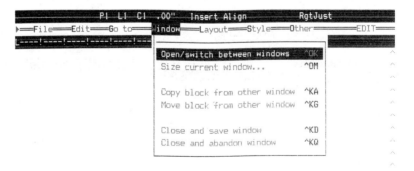

Layout Menu

The Layout menu has a variety of commands, including dot commands, that affect the paging and formatting of your document.

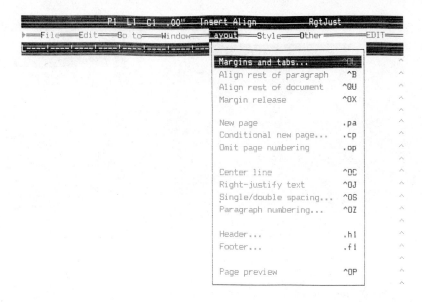

Style Menu

The Style menu deals with the special print controls and fonts plus the screen display of these functions.

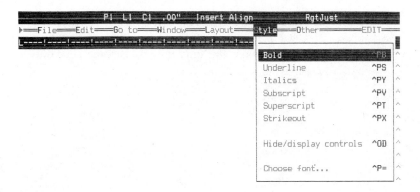

Other Menu

Finally the Other menu allows selection of the supplemental programs that work in conjunction with WordStar.

EXERCISES

1. Type Example 16. Return to the beginning of the file and scroll through the file using the Repeat command. Try various speeds.

2. Use the Interrupt command to stop the scrolling in Exercise 1.

3. Display the various menus discussed in this lesson. In particular, if you are familiar with only one type of menu, pull-down or traditional, take the time now to become acquainted with the other type.

Example 16

```
         SUGGESTIONS FOR COMPUTER CONFIGURATION AND USE IN M.U.S.D.

CLASSROOM I                  Formal Programming Class
                             6 Stations, Printer (High Quality)
                             Dual Disk
                             Word Processing

CLASSROOM II                 Formal Programming, CAI
                             6 Stations Printer (High Speed)
                             Dual Disk
                             Open for Individual Teachers

ADMINISTRATION               Two Stations: Printer
                             Dual Disk - Hard Disk
                             Word Processing

MOBIL UNIT                   4 Stations to be used in various class-
                             rooms and schools for short periods

USES:

1.  TEACH:      a.  Basic Programming      - All Students
                b.  Assembly Language      - MGM
                c.  Word Processing        - Business Students
                d.  Accounting(Bookkeeping) - Business Students
                e.  Computer "Literacy"    - Bus. & Gen. Students
                f.  Special Projects       - e.g., Plotter
                g.  Journalism             - English Students

2.  Computer Assisted Instruction (CAI)
        Useful in all areas - particularly for remedial work.

3.  ADMINISTRATION:
        a.  Attendance (H.S.)*       f. Physical Performance Test*
        b.  Attendance & State Reports  g. WASC*
            (elem.)*                 h. District Handbook
        c.  Scholarships*            i. District Directory
        d.  Voc. Ed. (records)*      j. Reports
        e.  OWE (records)*           k. Recordkeeping (misc.)

While building towards the desired computer facilities in the
school district, careful planning should be maintained to ensure
maximum compatibility of software between systems.

*Projects completed or in progress.
```

17

MERGE PRINTING— LETTERS WITH A DATA FILE

Merge printing is a powerful addition to WordStar's primary function, word processing. Merge printing allows you to generate form letters with names, addresses, or other information automatically inserted in the format you wish. In general, the information comes from a data file or is entered from the keyboard at the appropriate time. There are also four predefined variables available for merge printing. Let's look first at these.

PREDEFINED VARIABLES

The four predefined variables that can be accessed are shown here.

Variable	Function
&@&	Inserts the date maintained by DOS
&!&	Inserts the time maintained by DOS
&#&	Inserts the current page number
&__&	Inserts the current line number

Note that the symbols (@ and !) for the predefined variables time and date are the same as those on the Shorthand menu for these functions. If your computer system has a battery-operated clock, the date and time are automatically set. If not, be sure to set the date and time correctly before using either of these variables.

Using &#& places the page number at the position of the variable, not just in the footer or header.

These variables may be used in any document file. The only requirement is that when you print, you must select M (for Merge print) from the opening menu instead of P (for Print). Only Merge print inserts data from another file or data entered from the keyboard while printing. For example, you may use the date variable with a memo heading, as shown in the following example. It automatically prints the correct date in place of the variable &@&.

```
                         MEMO


        TO:   Jack Martinez      DATE:   &@&

        FROM: John Brown         RE:   Computer Systems
```

PRINTING USING
A DATA FILE

To merge information from a data file into a document, you'll need two files:

1. A master document that contains the text and instructions for the information that will be inserted.

2. A data file, a nondocument file containing all the information to be inserted in the master document.

A variety of options are available with Merge print, allowing you to control what information from your data file is inserted into your master document, the format of that data, and the format of the final document.

There are a few symbols and dot commands used only for merge printing. They will be introduced in this and the next two chapters. For this chapter we will use

Command	Function
.DF	Specifies data file name
.RV	Assigns variable names
&	Inserts variable data
/O	Omits line with no data

NONDOCUMENT DATA FILE

To see how merge printing works, let's enter a mailing list and a form letter to be sent to each name on the list.

Let's begin by creating a data file. All of the files we have created so far with WordStar have been document files. Load WordStar and select **N** to open a nondocument file. Name the file NAMES3.DTA and press ENTER. Note that the status line for a nondocument file is different from that of a document file.

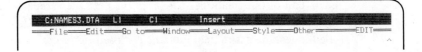

```
C:NAMES3.DTA   L1      C1          Insert
===File===Edit===Go to===Window===Layout===Style===Other=========EDIT===
```

The disk drive and file name are shown in the same manner as for a document file. L1 indicates the cursor is in line number 1, and C1 tells you the cursor is on column 1. Notice the extension used for the file name. It's a good idea to distinguish data files with a special extension such as .DTA, as used here. It helps prevent them from being confused with the master document.

In nondocument mode word wrap is not available to you. This is necessary so that no unintentional spaces (soft spaces) or carriage returns are entered into the file. Starting on line 1, column 1, enter the data from Example 17A just as it appears. Be sure to use exactly the same punctuation and spacing and to end each line, including the last, by pressing ENTER.

Let's take a look at one record in this data file. A record is a collection of related items; in this case, it is all the data on one individual. Each of the lines in the record contains the same type of information or at least a place for the information. This organization should be consistent from record to record in the same data file. The data in the first record is listed here. The space allocated for each item in the record is called a *field*.

Title:	Mr.
First name:	HENRY
Last name:	RATH
Number and street:	123 SACK ST.
Apartment number:	APT. 6
City, State, ZIP:	"CONCORD, CA 94520"
Telephone number:	(415)229-6251
Profession:	legal

Each item of information, or field, in the data file is separated by a comma, and if an individual field contains a comma as the City, State, ZIP field does, the entire field must be enclosed in quotation marks as shown in the list. Also notice that the first record, the data for Henry Rath, includes an apartment number. The next two records (for Ballew and Carlson) do not include apartment numbers, but you must still enter a comma in each record (with no space around it) to maintain the position of all of the data items. Every record in a data file *must* have the same number of fields. The most common error in working with merge printing is to be short a field or have an extra field in a record.

If the records you create are longer than will fit on the screen, you may place them on two lines for easier viewing. To do this, end a field with ENTER instead of a comma (not both). Never press ENTER in the middle of a field. For example, after the entry **Mr.** you can press ENTER, but you cannot press ENTER in the middle of "Walnut Creek, CA." Also, do not place any dot commands in a data file, unless, of course, they are items in a record. Inspect the file you just typed to be sure all commas and quotation marks are in the proper places. Save the file in the normal manner using ^KD.

One final note: The comma is the default field separator; you can use another symbol — asterisk (*), number sign (#), or whatever you like — so long as you indicate to WordStar what it is when the .DF command is used. The .DF command is discussed next.

MASTER DOCUMENT

Now we need the master document. Type Example 17B as a document file with the name POLIT1.MD. The purpose of each of the new dot commands will be discussed shortly. Again, adding a special extension for a master document is worthwhile. When you generate master documents, you must consider two areas a little differently than when you generate single-print documents. First, you must consider page numbering. Because it is assumed you are going to print the text of your file more than once, you can use either .OP or .PN to control page numbering. Entering .OP omits page numbers altogether, which is appropriate for a single-page letter. If your document is more than one page long and you want page numbers printed starting with page 1 each time the file is printed, you must enter .PN 1. As usual, you should enter the command at the beginning of the file, before you enter any text.

Second, you must consider page breaks. Be sure the .PA command is included at the end of your file so that printing of each subsequent letter begins on a new page.

DATA FILE NAME (.DF)

Use .DF to tell WordStar the name of the data file to get data from—in this example, the name of the data file you entered previously (NAMES3.DTA). Normally .DF is used just as shown in Example 17B. If you use a separator other than a comma in your data file, then you must indicate the separator after the .DF command (for example, entering .DF NAMES3.DTA,# tells WordStar that the number sign is used to separate fields in the data file NAMES3.DTA).

READ VARIABLE (.RV)

The .RV dot command is always used in conjunction with .DF. It is used to assign variable names to each of the items in a data file record. These variable names must be listed in the same order as the information fields are within the data file records. Type **.RV**, a space, and then each variable name separated by commas. This example is from Example 17B.

```
.OP
.DF NAMES3.DTA
.RV TITLE,FNAME,LNAME,STREET,APT,CITY,PHONE,PROF
```

Avoid using commas, spaces, or other punctuation as part of a variable name. Each variable name may contain up to 39 characters (letters and numbers).

INSERTION POINT (&)

A pair of ampersands (&) is used to indicate where data from the data file should be inserted into a printed document. Enclosed within each pair of ampersands is one of the variable names from the .RV command line.

Variable names correspond to the data in each field of the data record in the data file. When a document is printed, Merge print inserts the information from the corresponding data field in place of the variable name in the master document. You don't have to use the data from every field in the data file in your master document. (You *must* have a variable name entered in the .RV statement to correspond to each field of data in the data file being used. This keeps data in the proper order and allows you to use the same data file with different master documents.)

When the first letter is printed, the data from the fields in the first record of the data file will be substituted for their corresponding variables. When the second document is printed, the data from the fields of the second record will be substituted, and so on. The number of records in a data file is limited only by disk space.

OMIT BLANK LINES (/O)

In the master document, the insertion command for the variable APT (apartment) contains the characters /O. This tells Merge print that if there is no data for this item, as is the case in the second and third records, do not leave a blank line. The /O characters must appear within the ampersand insertion characters for that variable. An example of the output with and without using the /O characters is shown here.

```
&FNAME& &LNAME&          Kat Ballew
&STREET&                 6880 Walnut Blvd.
&APT&
&CITY&                   Walnut Creek, CA   94598


&FNAME& &LNAME&          Kat Ballew
&STREET&                 6880 Walnut Blvd.
&APT/O&                  Walnut Creek, CA   94598
&CITY&
```

PRINTING A MERGE PRINT FILE

To print the example file with Merge print, be sure the data file and the document file are on the logged subdirectory or that the appropriate disk and subdirectory identifier precedes their file names.

From the opening menu, select M, Merge print a file. You are presented with the Merge print dialog box shown in the following illustration.

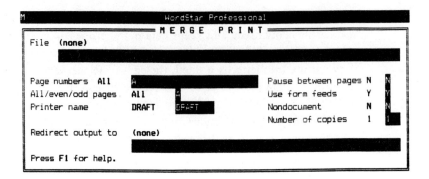

The questions shown in this illustration are the same as those in the Print dialog box. Select the file name POLIT1.MD and press ENTER. Give your desired response for each question or press ESC to give the default responses to each question. Merge print will print the form letter for each person in your data file. (If you requested multiple copies, it will print that number of copies of each letter.) A sample letter, with the data from record two, is shown in Example 17C.

CALCULATING WHILE
MERGE PRINTING (.MA)

WordStar also lets you solve mathematical problems while merge printing by using the dot command .MA. This dot command allows you access to all the math functions available in calculator mode. The format for the math dot command (.MA) is

.MA *variable* = *equation*

With a simple equation, the command looks like this:

.MA SUM = &purchase1& + &purchase2& + &purchase3&

A comma may be used in place of the equal sign, as shown here:

.MA SUM,&purchase1& + &purchase2& + &purchase3&

Note that the variables to the right of the equal sign (or comma) are enclosed by ampersands (&), and the variable to the left is not (the variables on the right need data substituted into them and therefore require ampersands). When you merge print, the data file is read, information is substituted for the variables, calculations are performed, and the result is printed in your text in place of the variable &SUM&.

A sample master document and data file using the .MA command is shown here.

```
.OP
.DF PURCHASE.DTA
.RV PURCHASE1,PURCHASE2,PURCHASE3
.MA SUM=&PURCHASE1&+&PURCHASE2&+&PURCHASE3&
.MA TOTAL = .065*&SUM&+&SUM&
Mr. John Smith
789 Pine Street
Martinez, CA  94553

Dear Mr. Smith:

Your purchases for May were &PURCHASE1&, &PURCHASE2&, and
&PURCHASE3&.  The total of your purchases was &SUM&.  With tax
your bill comes to &TOTAL&.

Sincerely,


Jack Super
-----------------------------------------------------------------
PURCHASE.DTA data

19.31,33.14,21.56
```

The output using these two files is shown here.

```
Mr. John Smith
789 Pine Street
Martinez, CA  94553

Dear Mr. Smith:

Your purchases for May were 19.31, 33.14, and 21.56.  The total
of your purchases was 74.01.  With tax your bill comes to
78.82065.

Sincerely,


Jack Super
```

The number format can be made to fit your needs better than this example shows, as you'll see in the next lesson.

EXERCISES

1. Add the appropriate data for three more people to the NAMES3.DTA file. From the opening menu, rename the file NAMES6.DTA.

2. Using the political contributions letter, merge print the file using NAMES6.DTA to verify that all the data was entered correctly. Use the predefined data variable &@& to enter the current date.

Example 17A

```
Mr.,HENRY,RATH,123 SACK ST.,APT. 6,"CONCORD, CA  94520",(415) 229-6251,legal
Mr.,KAT.BALLEW,6880 WALNUT BLVD.,,"WALNUT CREEK, CA  94598",(415) 698-3320,medical
Ms.,EFFIE,CARLSON,214 MIDHILL DR.,,"MARTINEZ, CA  95443",(415) 228-3006, teaching
```

Example 17B

```
.OP
.DF NAMES3.MRG
.RV TITLE,FNAME,LNAME,STREET,APT,CITY,PHONE,PROF



                DESERT SPRINGS COUNTY SUPERVISORS OFFICE
                   COUNTY BUILDING - SUITE 3001A
                      2105 WEST ACACIA BLVD.
                 DESERT SPRINGS, CALIFORNIA  94562
                         (707) 324-9109

                         July 9, 1982



&TITLE& &FNAME& &LNAME&
&STREET&
&APT/O&
&CITY&

Dear &TITLE& &LNAME&:

In my three terms serving as your County Supervisor, I hope my
honest support of the &PROF& profession has earned your trust and
your vote.  More than that &TITLE& &LNAME& I hope you can see
your way clear to the modest campaign contribution of $25.00 tax
deductible dollars.


Sincerely,



Jerome P. Hunnycutt
County Supervisor

JH:sb
.PA
```

Example 17C

```
            DESERT SPRINGS COUNTY SUPERVISORS OFFICE
                  COUNTY BUILDING - SUITE 3001A
                     2105 WEST ACACIA BLVD.
                DESERT SPRINGS, CALIFORNIA  94562
                       (707) 324-9109

                        July 9, 1982



    Mr. KAT BALLEW
    6880 WALNUT BLVD.
    WALNUT CREEK, CA  94598


    Dear Mr. BALLEW:

    In my three terms serving as your County Supervisor, I hope my
    honest support of the medical profession has earned your trust
    and your vote.  More than that Mr. BALLEW I hope you can see your
    way clear to the modest campaign contribution of $25.00 tax
    deductible dollars.


    Sincerely,



    Jerome P. Hunnycutt
    County Supervisor

    JH:sb
```

18

MERGE PRINTING — FORM LETTERS FORMATTING, AND CONDITIONAL COMMANDS

In Lesson 17, the source of the data used for merge printing was a data file. You can also enter variable data into form letters directly from the keyboard while they are being printed. To accomplish this, you will use the following new dot commands in this lesson:

Command	Function
.AV	Asks for variable
.CS	Clears screen
.DM	Displays message
.SV	Sets variable

KEYBOARD DATA ENTRY

To enter data from the keyboard while merge printing a document, you will find it convenient to enter a series of commands. In effect, these commands tell WordStar to take data from the keyboard rather than from the data file. (You can enter data from the keyboard, plus get data from a data file, in the same document.) Let's work with the POLIT1.MD file from Lesson 17.

Suppose you want to vary the contribution requested from $25 to some other value based on the person's profession, past contributions, or some other factor. At the beginning of the file, just after the .RV command, enter the following:

```
.CS
.DM  Contribution  request  from:  &LNAME& — profession:&
PROF&
.AV "Amount of Contribution?",AMOUNT
```

Let's look at each of these variables in turn.

CLEAR SCREEN (.CS)

Generally it is appropriate to use Merge print's Clear Screen command (.CS) prior to using the .AV command (discussed shortly). If .CS is placed in your file ahead of .AV, then each time Merge print asks for data to be entered, the request will be made on a clear screen. This is particularly useful when there are several keyboard entries for each letter you are merge printing.

To refresh your memory as to what information is required, you can enter a message after the .CS command, such as **.CS Enter data as requested.**

DISPLAY MESSAGE (.DM)

The .DM command allows you to display a message without first clearing the screen, but the normal procedure is to use it following .CS. This message may include variable names from the .RV command line. In the example above &LNAME& is used to display the last name and &PROF& the profession of the individual you are requesting the contribution from.

ASK FOR VARIABLE (.AV)

The .AV command specifies the variable to be entered from the keyboard. As when you use a data file, when merge print reaches the .AV variable name, it replaces that variable name with actual data. The difference is that you must enter that data from the keyboard, rather than have it automatically entered from the data file.

In the .AV line we entered the variable name AMOUNT. This variable must also be entered in the document file, bracketed by & characters to identify it as an insertion variable. In the text of the letter, now replace $25.00 with **&AMOUNT&.**

When you print this file, Merge print will know that AMOUNT is a variable and that it should *ask* for that data. It "asks" by printing a message on the screen, prompting you to enter the data. The message it prints is the message you typed following the .AV command—in this case, "Amount of contribution?" This message *must* be enclosed in quotation marks and have a comma separating it from the variable name.

When you enter this variable's data, you are limited to the number of characters that will take you to the end of the line on your screen.

Note: Depending on the characteristics of your printer, the point in your file where the printer is stopped may not appear to coincide with the data you are entering. Enter data according to the prompt messages. WordStar will print the document as formatted in the master document. If you have more than one variable to "ask" for in a letter, each variable should be entered on a separate .AV command line. For example, if you enter the commands

.AV NAME
.AV TITLE

when you merge print, you will enter data on the screen as follows (the program prompts you with the variable name):

NAME? **Jennifer** ENTER
TITLE? **TEACHER** ENTER

Run POLIT1.MD now entering appropriate values.

SET VARIABLE (.SV)

Another useful merge print command is .SV, for set variable. It has two functions: it specifies a variable to hold a constant value during merge printing, and it controls formatting.

In the current example the name and address are changed for each letter. But there are situations where either a variable will be the same for several letters, or the same variable might change several times in the same letter.

Take a look at Example 13 from Lesson 13. In a will, the same names normally occur several times. In place of the actual names, the variables NAME1, NAME2, and so forth, can be substituted. The .SV command is used at the beginning of the file to identify the actual name that should replace each variable in the text. You can then type the names once, and they will be changed throughout the document. Each variable must be entered with a separate .SV command.

Note: Any time something is centered, as is the name in the will heading, you can use the centering format variable discussed in the next section.

While merge printing, you can automatically format both text and numeric data. To set up either text or numeric format strings, you use the dot command .SV, set variable. We'll consider text formatting first and then number formatting.

FORMATTING TEXT

You can left align, right align, or center text using the letters L, R, and C, respectively. The first step is to define the format string with .SV. For example,

```
.SV 1 = LLLLLL
```

```
          L> Format string; sets the length and  justifies
             the text left(L), right(R), or center(C)

        L>    Variable name (any single number or  letter  except
              the letter O)

   L>  The .SV dot command; defines the format string
```

Text formatting follows these rules:

- In the first position of the format string, enter **R** to right justify, **L** to left justify, and **C** to center text within the format string.

- Any other characters, including spaces, will print in the position they appear.

- The number of characters in the format string determines the number of spaces available for the variable.

- Excess characters—those on the right for left justification and those on the left for right justification—will be cut off.

- Other characters or spaces add to the string length and will print literally, even if there are characters for that position.

In the following example, the format strings are labeled A, B, C, and 1. Format strings A and B are too short to hold the name George Washington. Notice how it is shortened in each case. Format string C is the same length as the ruler line, 65 characters, and will center the text on a ruler line of that length. Format string 1 is presented to illustrate the masking effect of the characters other than L, R, and C, in the format string.

Enter and print the following master document and data file to verify the results.

```
.HE TEXT.MD

.OP
.DF TEXT.DTA
.RV VAR1,VAR2,VAR3
.SV A = LLLLLLLLLLLLLL
.SV B = RRRRRRRRRRRRRR
.SV C = CCCCCCCCCCCCCCCCCCCCCCCCCCCCCCCCCCCCCCCCCCCCCCCCCCCCCCCCCCCCC
.SV 1 = LLABLL

&VAR1/A&
&VAR1/B&
&VAR1/C&

&VAR3/A&
&VAR1/C&

&VAR2/1&


---------------------------------------------------------------
TEXT.DTA data:

George Washington,123456,Hello
```

The output produced by the two files is shown here.

```
George Washing
rge Washington
                              George Washington

Hello
                              George Washington

12AB56
```

FORMATTING NUMBERS

Numbers are always right justified when printed, but a variety of formatting options are available to control various characters that are printed with numbers.

Here are the format symbols available.

Symbol	Function
9	Substitutes a digit in place of each 9. If no digit is available, a zero is substituted. If you use the format string 99999.99, the number 231.40, for example, will be displayed as 00231.40.
Z	Substitutes a digit in place of each Z. If there is no digit, a space is substituted. If you use the format string ZZZZZ.ZZ, the number 231.40 will be displayed as (2 spaces)231.40.
*	Substitutes a digit in place of each asterisk. If no digit is available, an asterisk is substituted. After a decimal point, a zero is substituted. If you use the format string *****.**, the number 231.40 will be displayed as **231.40, and the number 231 will be displayed as **231.00.
$	Substitutes a digit in place of each $, if not a leading zero. Places a $ to the left of the first digit. If you use the format string $$$$$$.99 the number 231.40 will be displayed as (2 spaces)$231.40.
—	Places a minus sign before the leading digit of a negative number.
.	Places a decimal point in the position shown. If you use the format string 99999.999, the number 231.40 will be displayed as 231.400.
,	Places a comma in the position shown. If you use the format string 99,999.99, the number 1231.40 will be displayed as (1 space)1,231.40.
()	Places parentheses around negative numbers. If you use the format string ($$$$.99), the number −231.40 will be displayed as ($231.40).

These number formatting symbols can be used individually or in combination.

Following are a master document, the data file used by that document, and the output of the merged files. Experiment with these files to be sure your format strings behave the way you expect them to. Here is the master document.

```
.OP

Format examples:

.SV1= 9999999.99
.SV2= ZZZZZZZ.ZZ
.SV3= $999999.99
.SV4= -$*****.**
.SV5= 999,999.99
.SV6= ($$$$$$.99)
.DF FORMAT.DTA
.RV DATA1,DATA2,DATA3

Data being used:
```

&DATA1&	&DATA2&	&DATA3&
&DATA1/1&	&DATA2/1&	&DATA3/1&
&DATA1/2&	&DATA2/2&	&DATA3/2&
&DATA1/3&	&DATA2/3&	&DATA3/3&
&DATA1/4&	&DATA2/4&	&DATA3/4&
&DATA1/5&	&DATA2/5&	&DATA3/5&
&DATA1/6&	&DATA2/6&	&DATA3/6&

Next is the data file used by the master document.

```
------------------------------------------------------------

FORMAT.DTA data:

231.40,2165.5678,-7954.12
```

Finally, here is the output produced by the master document.

```
Format examples:


Data being used:
      231.40              2165.5678            -7954.12
    0000231.40           0002165.56          0007954.12
       231.40              2165.56             7954.12
   $000231.40           $002165.56          $007954.12
   ***$231.40           **$2165.56          *-$7954.12
   000 231.40            002,165.56          007,954.12
      $231.40              $2165.56          ($7954.12)
```

CONDITIONAL COMMANDS

Powerful additions to WordStar's merge printing capabilities are the conditional commands. These allow you to use the same master document to print a variety of material, depending on the conditions you set. For example, you can send a letter to only those individuals on your mailing list whose ZIP codes fall within a particular range.

The conditional commands have a wide variety of applications. We will look at an example after all four commands and their formats have been introduced.

THE IF CONDITION (.IF)

The dot command .IF is generally used to compare two items: If the comparison is true, then one operation is performed; if the comparison is false, then another operation is performed. To compare two items, you need an operator such as an equal sign. The operators recognized by the dot command .IF are divided into two categories: text operators and numeric operators, as shown here.

Text operators

Operator	Meaning
=	Is the same as (alphabetically)
<	Comes before (alphabetically)
>	Comes after (alphabetically)
<=	Comes before or is the same as (alphabetically)
>=	Comes after or is the same as (alphabetically)
<>	Is not the same as (alphabetically)

Numerical operators

Operator	Meaning
#=	Is equal to (numerically)
#>	Is greater than (numerically)
#<	Is less than (numerically)
#>=	Is greater than or equal to (numerically)
#<=	Is less than or equal to (numerically)
#<>	Is not equal to (numerically)

You can use these operators to compare two variables or a variable and a constant; for example,

.IF &purchase1& > &purchase2&

or

.IF &purchase1& #> 500

If the comparison is true, one operation is performed; if it is false, another operation is performed.

THE ELSE CONDITION (.EL)

The dot command .EL gives you the opportunity to kill two birds with one stone, so to speak. Consider this example:

.IF &JOB& = D

Text of letter sent to doctors

.EL

Text of letter sent to lawyers

.EI

In this example, the data file has a field to identify whether the record holds the data for a doctor or a lawyer. If the record contains data for a doctor, signified by the letter D, the letter directed specifically toward doctors is printed. If the record contains data for a lawyer (anything but a D is in the field), control is passed to the text following the .EL command, then a letter directed specifically toward lawyers is sent.

THE END IF CONDITION (.EI)

The .IF dot command is normally followed by the text to be printed if the condition is true. If the condition is false, control proceeds to the next dot command — which may be another .IF command or, more likely, the End If command, .EI. When all the IF conditions have been tested, an .EI command *must* terminate the process.

THE GO COMMAND (.GO)

The Go command allows you to bypass a portion of the text in the master document if a condition is met.

In the following example, when the IF condition is true, control passes to the end of the file, bypassing a section of text. If the IF condition is false, that section of text will be printed.

```
.IF &INCOME&< 4000
.GO bottom
.EI
```

Entering **.GO** t or **.GO T** is the same as entering **.GO TOP**, and **.GO** b or **.GO B** is the same as entering **.GO BOTTOM**.

USING CONDITIONAL COMMANDS

Let's try some of these commands in a master document. The following example directs different letters to people, depending on the town in which they reside.

```
.OP
.DF NAMES6.DTA
.RV TITLE,FNAME,LNAME,STREET,APT,CITY,ZIP,PHONE,PROF
.IF &ZIP& #= 94553
As a resident of Martinez. . .&TITLE& &FNAME& &LNAME&
.EI
.IF &ZIP& #= 94598
As a resident of Walnut Creek . . .&TITLE& &FNAME& &LNAME&
.EI
.IF &ZIP& #= 94520
As a resident of Pleasant Hill . . . &TITLE& &FNAME& &LNAME&
.EI
```

To keep from entering a completely new file, the NAMES6.DTA has been modified by placing the ZIP code in its own field. Note also the change in the .RV line above. The variable ZIP has been added.

```
Mr.,HENRY,RATH,123 SACK ST.,APT. 6,"PLEASANT HILL, CA",94520,(415) 229-6251,legal
Mr.,KAT BALLEW,6880 WALNUT BLVD.,,"WALNUT CREEK, CA",94598,(415) 698-3320,medical
Ms.,EFFIE,CARLSON,214 MIDHILL DR.,,"MARTINEZ, CA",94553,(415) 228-3006,teaching
Mr.,RALPH,KNIGHT,370 MAIN ST.,,"PLEASANT HILL, CA",94520,(415) 378-5567,teaching
Mr.,CARL,CARLSON,989 PEACH BLVD.,,"PLEASANT HILL, CA",94520,(415) 228-2459,medical
Mr.,GEORGE,GODFREY,1891 ALHAMBRA AVE.,,"MARTINEZ, CA",94553,(415) 372-6483,legal
```

In the previous lesson you were asked to produce this file by adding three names to NAMES3.DTA. Change your data structure to match the preceding illustration. An example of output from these files is shown here (the actual output will depend on your data).

```
As a resident of Pleasant Hill . . . Mr. HENRY RATH
As a resident of Walnut Creek . . .Mr. KAT BALLEW
As a resident of Martinez. . .Ms. EFFIE CARLSON
As a resident of Pleasant Hill . . . Mr. RALPH KNIGHT
As a resident of Pleasant Hill . . . Mr. CARL CARLSON
As a resident of Martinez. . .Mr. GEORGE GODFREY
```

CHECKING DATA FILES

It is very easy to inadvertently add an extra comma in a data record and thereby add an extra field to a record. All information inserted in a file after that error would then come from the wrong field. The same problem would occur if you leave out a comma, thus omitting a field.

One way to check a file for this type of error is to place a dummy field at the end of each record. In that field you could place a special mark, such as an asterisk (*), or you could use the Shorthand menu to design a macro to print END and place that in the last field. Then if you write a master document to print the last field of each record, if anything but the * or END (or whatever you placed there) is printed, you know there is an error, and the data that is printed shows you where the error is. You can then quickly edit and correct the data file.

As an illustration of this idea, let's place END at the end of each record using a shorthand macro. We'll use E with ESC to invoke the macro, and make END the definition displayed. The WordStar command to move the cursor to the end of the record, print a comma, print END, and move the cursor to the line below is $^\wedge$QD,END,$^\wedge$X. Remember, when entering shorthand macros, you must precede CTRL commands with $^\wedge$P. If you enter this information in the Shorthand menu, it will display with the "MENU & KEY DEFINITION" as:

```
MENU & KEY DEFINITIONS   Bytes available: 496
E    END
      ^QD,END^X
```

Now you can place END at the end of a new record in a data file or at the end of each record in an existing file just by pressing ESC **E**. This was done with the file NAMES6.DTA used in the previous section. The sample master document shown here was then used to print END, the last item of each record.

```
.df names6.dta
.rv title,fname,lname,address,apt,city,zip,telephone,prof,end
&END&
```

To show the effect of omitting a comma, one was deleted in the second record of NAMES6.DTA. Then Merge print was used to obtain the following printout:

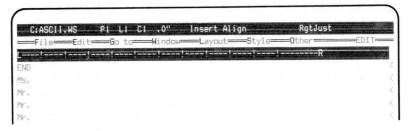

The data in this illustration was first output to a disk and then opened as a WordStar file in nondocument mode. This procedure is discussed in the following section.

PRINTING TO DISK

Experimenting with WordStar's merge commands and checking data files can consume a lot of paper. To avoid wasting paper, you can write the output from your practice files to your disk. This also saves a lot of time because writing to a disk is a lot faster than printing. After the file is written to the disk, open the file with WordStar and examine its contents.

You have three ways to print the output of a file to a disk. With the PRINT menu displayed, advance the cursor to the "Printer Name" field. The directory of printer drivers displays at the bottom of the screen. You can select one of the options that prints to the disk. These options (if they weren't dropped in the installation process) are ASCII, PRVIEW, and XTRACT. Their functions are listed here.

Driver	Function
ASCII	Produces a disk file with all dot commands and print controls removed. Each line ends with a carriage return.

PRVIEW   Produces a disk file similar to the printer output. Headers, footers, and special print functions are displayed where possible. Data is inserted if merge-printing is used. Hard carriage returns are used.

XTRACT   Output is similar to PRVIEW's but no headers or footers are included. Soft carriage returns are retained so that some editing can be done with WordStar.

Each of these drivers names the disk file with its name plus the extension WS (that is, ASCII.WS, PRVIEW.WS, or XTRACT.WS). If you want to save the file, be sure to change the name before the next save operation. You will have to experiment with the disk save options to see which is best for the file output you are working with.

EXERCISES

1. Print the political contributions letters set up in this lesson, entering the contribution amount from the keyboard and setting the date with the predefined date variable. Use the .SV command to define the appropriate format string for the contribution. *Hint:* The dot commands and a keyboard entry sequence are shown in Example 18A.

2. Print the political contributions letter from Lesson 17, but this time enter names and addresses from the keyboard instead of from a data file.

3. Print the will from Lesson 13, entering the name of the deceased and friend only once. Example 18B shows the dot commands and three sections of the document file. Note that you must select M, Merge print, to print this document, rather than the regular Word-Star print function.

4. Add appropriate format strings to the bill sent to Mr. Smith in Lesson 17, so that the dollar amounts are printed in the proper format.

5. Revise the master document that prints the bill to Mr. Smith so that it is sent to the people in your NAMES6.DTA file with a given ZIP code. You will have to add purchase data to each record.

Example 18A

```
.OP
.DF NAMES3.DTA
.RV TITLE,FNAME,LNAME,STREET,APT,CITY,PHONE,PROF
.SV DATE, July 9, 1987
.CS
.DM Contribution request for:  &LNAME&, profession - &PROF&
.AV "Amount of contribution ?",AMOUNT
```

```
 C:EXAMPLE.18A      P01      #01
═════════════════════ P R I N T I N G ═════════════════════
    P pause                          ^U cancel printing
    C continue after pausing         F print at full speed
    B print from background
```

```
Contribution request for:   , profession -
Amount of contribution ?
```

Example 18B

```
.PN 1
.SV NAME1, JOHN PHILIP SMITH
.SV NAME2, MARCY SIMMONS
```

                    LAST WILL AND TESTAMENT

                              OF

                      JOHN PHILIP SMITH

I, &NAME1&, presently residing in the City of Walnut Creek, Contra Costa County, California, being of sound and disposing mind and memory, and not acting under duress, menace, or undue influence of any kind or person whatsoever, do hereby make, publish and declare this to be my Last Will and Testament in the following manner:

                          ARTICLE V

I give, devise and bequeath one-half (1/2) of the residue of my estate, real, personal, or mixed, of whatever kind and wheresoever situated to my very good friend, &NAME2&, and then to her issue by right of representation. If &NAME2& shall predecease me, this gift shall lapse.

                          ARTICLE VII

I hereby nominate and request the court to appoint my friend, &NAME2&, as Executrix of this Will, to serve without bond. Should &NAME2& serve as Executrix, I authorize her to sell, lease, convey, transfer, encumber, hypothecate, or otherwise deal with the whole or any portion of my estate, either by public or private sale, with or without notice, and without securing any prior order of the court therefor.

19

MERGE PRINTING— SPECIAL PRINTING, CHAINING, AND NESTING

WordStar 5 gives you merge printing capabilities using data files created with WordStar, MailList, Lotus 1-2-3, Symphony, dBase, and Quattro. This lesson discusses only documents and data files created with WordStar.

Some master documents are presented in this Merge Print lesson, using a combination of the commands introduced in the two previous lessons, as well as two new commands.

At times you will create a master document to direct printing from a data file, a document file, or both. This lesson introduces the command that allows this operation. It also presents the command for controlling print-time formatting. These commands are summarized here.

Command	Function
.FI	Insert files
.PF	Control formatting

FILE INSERT (.FI)

The File Insert command (.FI) is used to perform two functions: chaining and nesting. You can create a master document using a series of .FI commands to select a series of files to print. This process is called *chaining*. You can also use the .FI command to insert the text of one file into the text of another. This process is referred to as *nesting*.

Two examples of chaining are shown here. Each example shows how the master document file appears on the screen. Pay particular attention to the symbols in the flag column. Notice that ENTER is pressed twice to separate each File Insert command. A final ENTER should follow the last .FI command.

The first example shows the simplest form of a master document using the File Insert command. The three files are printed continuously with only a single line between the files.

For the second example, open a master document file and name it **PRINTDOC.MD.** Enter the text shown here.

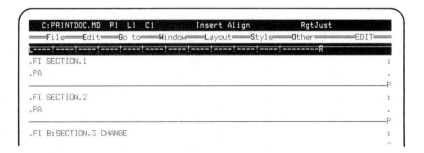

Notice that this file has two additional features. First, .PA is placed between the File Insert commands so that each section printed will begin on a new page. Second, CHANGE is added after SECTION.3 to allow you to change the disk in drive B before SECTION.3 is printed, which you will want to do when the files you are printing reside on more than one floppy disk. The printer will stop after SECTION.2 is printed, and the following message will be displayed:

.FI B:SECTION.3 CHANGE

Change disk. Press C when ready to continue

If you are using a floppy disk system, when WordStar is ready for you to reinsert the disk, it will present you with the appropriate message. The final section will then be printed.

Chaining and nesting may be performed by selecting either P or M from the File menu (or OPENING MENU) so long as variables will not be inserted into one or more of the files.

PRINT FORMATTING (.PF)

The print formatting command .PF can have any one of three settings; ON, OFF, or DIS. If you use .PF ON, formatting is performed throughout the file unless a section is specifically turned off with the .AW command. If you use .PF OFF, formatting is not performed. If you use the DIS (discretionary) option, formatting is performed only where merge printing variables are introduced.

PRINTING DATA FILES

The remainder of Lesson 19 uses a variety of Merge Print commands to show some practical applications of Merge printing. We will first look at an application that prints data files.

Enter the information from Example 19A into a data file with the name NAMES8.DTA (remember to select **N** for nondocument mode).

Nondocument files are usually difficult to read in the default format they display. By using the text formatting commands developed in Lesson 18, you can easily print whatever data you like in a very readable format. For the data file NAMES8.DTA, we'll print the name, phone number, and profession of each person listed in the file. We will also give the printout a heading.

Open a file with the name CONTRIB.MD and enter the following:

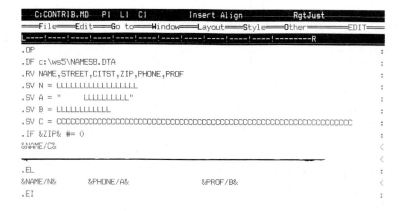

```
 C:CONTRIB.MD  P1  L1  C1           Insert Align          RgtJust
====File====Edit====Go to====Window====Layout====Style====Other====    ====EDIT====
!----!----!----!----!----!----!----!----!----!----!--------R
.OP                                                              :
.DF c:\ws5\NAMES8.DTA                                            :
.RV NAME,STREET,CITST,ZIP,PHONE,PROF                             :
.SV N = LLLLLLLLLLLLLLLLLL                                       :
.SV A = "        LLLLLLLLLL"                                      :
.SV B = LLLLLLLLLLL                                              :
.SV C = CCCCCCCCCCCCCCCCCCCCCCCCCCCCCCCCCCCCCCCCCCCCCCCCCCCCCCCCCCCCCCCC :
.IF &ZIP& #= 0                                                   :
&NAME/C&                                                         <

————————————————————————————————————————————————————————————————
.EL                                                              :
&NAME/N&         &PHONE/A&                 &PROF/B&              <
.EI                                                              :
```

Save the file. To print the heading, we'll add a new record at the top of the data file. With the cursor in the upper left corner (press HOME), insert a blank line and enter

85 CONTRIBUTORS,A,C,O,PHONE,PROF

Your file should look like the following illustration.

```
85 CONTRIBUTORS,A,C,O,PHONE,PROF
HENRY RATH,123 SACK ST.,"WALNUT CREEK, CA",94598,(415) 229-6251,legal
KAT BALLEW,6880 WALNUT BLVD.,"WALNUT CREEK, CA",94598,(415) 698-3320,medical
EFFIE CARLSON,214 MIDHILL DR.,"MARTINEZ, CA",94553,(415) 228-3006,teaching
RALPH KNIGHT,370 MAIN ST.,"PLEASANT HILL, CA",94520,(415) 378-5567,teaching
CARL CARLSON,989 PEACH BLVD.,"CONCORD, CA",94520,(415) 228-2459,medical
GEORGE GODFREY,1891 ALHAMBRA AVE.,"MARTINEZ, CA",94553,(415) 372-6483,legal
DAVID PEREZ,4830 PRIMROSE LN.,"PLEASANT HILL, CA",94520,(415) 698-5620,teaching
STEVE QUINN,659 FRANKLIN RD.,"WALNUT CREEK, CA",94598,(415) 229-6578,medical
```

The only portion printed is 85 CONTRIBUTORS. The 0 in the ZIP code field is used by WordStar to determine when the heading is printed. The data in other fields is just to help you verify there is data for each field. When you are through with this example, delete this heading record. You will use the same data to print mailing labels.

From the File menu press **M**, and use this master document, CONTRIB.MD, to read and print information in your data file. The output is shown here.

85 CONTRIBUTORS

HENRY RATH	229-6251	legal
KAT BALLEW	698-3320	medical
EFFIE CARLSON	228-3006	teaching
RALPH KNIGHT	378-5567	teaching
CARL CARLSON	228-2459	medical
GEORGE GODFREY	372-6483	legal
DAVID PEREZ	698-5620	teaching
STEVE QUINN	229-6578	medical

ADDRESSING ENVELOPES

Now we will write a file to direct envelope addressing. Open a document file with the name ENVELOPE.MD and enter the following:

```
.PL 33
.PO 5
JACK SMITH
150 MAIN ST
MARTINEZ, CA 94553
.PO 40
.DF NAMES3.DTA.
.RV TITLE,FNAME,LNAME,STREET,APT,CITY,PHONE,PROF
(3 blank lines)
&NAME&
&STREET&
&PT/O&
&CITY&
^P^C (This entry will appear as ^C on your screen.)
.PA
```

The .PL command sets the length for the envelopes. Choose a value so that the envelopes are released from the printer after each envelope is printed (.PL30 is equal to 5 inches).

Enter **.PO 5** to change the default page offset from 8/10 to 5/10 of an inch for correct placement of the return address. If you use envelopes with a preprinted return address, you should omit this command.

Enter **.PO 40** to place the address in the correct area of the envelope. Alternatively, you may place &TITLE&, &FNAME& &LNAME&, &STREET&, &APT&, and &CITY& in the proper column of your file, but the Page Offset command allows you to change easily to envelopes of different sizes.

Enter ^P^C, which will appear as ^C on your screen, to cause the printer to pause after each envelope is printed. This gives you time to insert the next envelope. If your printer has a sheet feeder with multiple bins, you would use the .BN command.

Try printing an envelope. Adjust the print commands as necessary to correctly align the addresses on your envelopes.

PRINTING LETTERS AND ENVELOPES

In this application of the File Insert command, we will print a form letter and address the envelopes. The printer will pause to allow insertion of letterhead and envelopes. To accomplish this, we will need four files: (1) a master document file to direct printing, (2) a form letter file, (3) an envelope printing file, and (4) a data file. Assemble these four files as follows on one disk.

1. Open a document file with the name LETENV.MD and enter the following:

   .FI POLIT1.MD

   (1 space)

   .FI ENVELOP2.MD

Don't forget to press ENTER after the second .FI command.
Save the file. It will control the printing of the letters and envelopes.

2. Edit the file POLIT1.MD so that the dot commands appear as follows:

   .OP

   .DF NAMES3.DTA

.RV TITLE, FNAME, LNAME, STREET, APT, CITY, PHONE,PROF

.CS

.DM INSERT LETTERHEAD

^P^C (Remember, only ^C appears on the screen.)

3. Open a file with the name ENVELOP2.MD and enter the following:

.OP

.PO 40

.DF NAMES3.DTA

.RV TITLE,FNAME,LNAME,STREET,APT,CITY,PHONE, PROF

.CS

.DM POSITION ENVELOPE TO PRINT ADDRESS IN PROPER POSITION

^P^C

(1 space)

&TITLE& &FNAME& &LNAME&

&STREET&

&APT/O&

&CITY&

Save the file. This will print an envelope for each form letter.

4. The data file NAMES3.DTA is unchanged from Lesson 18. With the four files complete, you are ready to print. Press **M** from the opening menu and Merge Print the LETENV.MD file. Appropriate prompts will be displayed when you are to insert letterhead or envelopes and when you should continue printing.

PRINTING MAILING LABELS

We will use the data file NAMES8.DTA with a master document to print mailing labels. Open a document file and name it ML.MD. Enter Example 19B as far as the last .RV dot command.

Before proceeding further, consider the portion of the example you have just entered. The .RR command establishes tab settings. You can adjust these later to fit your mailing labels. The .MT and .MB commands set the top and bottom margins to 0 because most mailing label forms are spaced evenly from one sheet to the next. The .DF command indicates the name of the file containing the data you are going to use. The next three lines contain .RV commands. We need three because we are going to print the labels three across. If the labels were two across, we would need two .RV command lines, and so on.

The variables in the first .RV line will hold the information from the first record of the data file, the second will hold .RV variables from the second record, and the third will hold .RV variables from the third record. This sequence will repeat itself, with the .RV commands gathering information from successive groups of three records as WordStar proceeds through the data file. Note that we did not have to distinguish the variables PHONE and PROF with numbers because this data is not being printed.

The .SV command is used to combine city, state, and ZIP code in a single format string. When the variables are printed, they all use the same format string (L). Also note that on the last three lines, the space between the variables is the same. The length of the L format string plus this space between variables adds up to the width of a mailing label.

Save the file and from the opening menu, press **M.** Merge print the ML.MD file; this will print the mailing labels. The format of sample printed labels is shown in Example 19C.

EXERCISES

1. Change your contribution file, CONTRIB.MD, to print addresses as well as the existing information.

2. Reprint the list of contributors using the conditional commands to limit it to those in the medical profession.

3. Create a master document file to address envelopes. Assume that the envelopes have a preprinted return address.

4. Create a master document to print four of your existing files in succession. If you work with a floppy disk system, use the change option in at least one .FI command.

5. Redo the mailing label example to suit the format of the mailing labels you use.

Example 19A

```
HENRY RATH,123 SACK ST.,"WALNUT CREEK, CA",94598,(415) 229-6251,legal
KAT BALLEW,6880 WALNUT BLVD.,"WALNUT CREEK, CA",94598,(415) 698-3320,medical
EFFIE CARLSON,214 MIDHILL DR.,"MARTINEZ, CA",94553,(415) 228-3006,teaching
RALPH KNIGHT,370 MAIN ST.,"PLEASANT HILL, CA",94520,(415) 378-5567,teaching
CARL CARLSON,989 PEACH BLVD.,"CONCORD, CA",94520,(415) 228-2459,medical
GEORGE GODFREY,1891 ALHAMBRA AVE.,"MARTINEZ, CA",94553,(415) 372-6483,legal
DAVID PEREZ,4830 PRIMROSE LN.,"PLEASANT HILL, CA",94520,(415) 698-5620,teaching
STEVE QUINN,659 FRANKLIN RD.,"WALNUT CREEK, CA",94598,(415) 229-6578,medical
```

Example 19B

```
.OP
.PF OFF
.PL 6
.MT 0
.MB 0
.PO 0
.SV L = LLLLLLLLLLLLLLLLLLLLLLLLLLLLLL
.DF NAMES8.DTA
.RV NAME1,STREET1,CITY1,ZIP1,PHONE,PROF
.RV NAME2,STREET2,CITY2,ZIP2,PHONE,PROF
.RV NAME3,STREET3,CITY3,ZIP3,PHONE,PROF
.SV CITYSTATEZIP1=&CITY1& &ZIP1&
.SV CITYSTATEZIP2=&CITY2& &ZIP2&
.SV CITYSTATEZIP3=&CITY3& &ZIP3&
&NAME1/L&        &NAME2/L&        &NAME3/L&
&STREET1/L&        &STREET2/L&        &STREET3/L&
&CITYSTATEZIP1/L&        &CITYSTATEZIP2/L&        &CITYSTATEZIP3/L&
```

Example 19C

```
HENRY RATH
123 SACK ST.
WALNUT CREEK, CA 94598

RALPH KNIGHT
370 MAIN ST.
PLEASANT HILL, CA 94520

DAVID PEREZ
4830 PRIMROSE LN.
PLEASANT HILL, CA 94520

KAT BALLEW
6880 WALNUT BLVD.
WALNUT CREEK, CA 94598

CARL CARLSON
989 PEACH BLVD.
CONCORD, CA 94520

STEVE QUINN
659 FRANKLIN RD.
WALNUT CREEK, CA 94598

EFFIE CARLSON
214 MIDHILL DR.
MARTINEZ, CA 94553

GEORGE GODFREY
1891 ALHAMBRA AVE.
MARTINEZ, CA 94553
```

LESSON

20

SPELLING CHECK
DICTIONARY
THESAURUS

WordStar 5 offers a dictionary in addition to a spelling checker and a thesaurus. All three features are integral parts of WordStar and very easy to use. Separate installation is not required.

SPELLING CHECK

The commands to access the spelling checker functions are listed here.

Command	Function
^QL	Checks the spelling in your document from the position of the cursor to the end of the file. To completely check a file, position the cursor at the beginning, before selecting ^QL. Words on dot command lines are not checked.
^QN	Checks the word at the position of the cursor. You can enter ^QN to check words on dot command lines. Also displays the definition of the word if one is available.

227

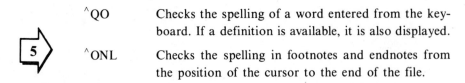

^QO	Checks the spelling of a word entered from the keyboard. If a definition is available, it is also displayed.
^ONL	Checks the spelling in footnotes and endnotes from the position of the cursor to the end of the file.

The first two commands, ^QL and ^QN, may be selected from the Other menu or by using the function keys. The default settings are SHIFT-F3 for ^QL and SHIFT-F4 for ^QN.

WordStar comes with a spelling checker that contains over 100,000 words, plus a supplemental personal spell checker to which you can add words. Initially, the personal dictionary has only one word, WordStar. The purpose of this personal dictionary is for you to add words that commonly occur in your work but that are not likely to be in the main dictionary. Some examples of such words are company names, names of people you deal with frequently, and products. Of course, be sure words are spelled correctly before you enter them. To delete words from your personal dictionary, open the file PERSONAL.DCT in nondocument mode and delete whatever words you like — files with the extension DCT do not appear in WordStar's directory.

When you enter ^QL, the spelling check starts immediately. When WordStar encounters a word that is not in one of the dictionaries, the spelling check stops, and the following Spelling Check menu is displayed.

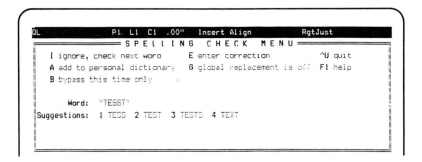

Let's look at each of the Spelling Check menu options.

Option	Result
I	Causes WordStar to ignore the word and other occurrences of the same word in the document. When you

are using $^\wedge$QL, the word is ignored and the cursor proceeds to the next word not found in the dictionary. When you are using $^\wedge$QN, the cursor moves to the next word in the file. When you are using $^\wedge$QO, you can enter a new word from the keyboard.

A   Adds the word to your personal dictionary. Once the word is in that dictionary, WordStar no longer stops at the word.

B   Causes WordStar to bypass the word this time but to stop at the next occurrence of the word.

E   Displays the Correction window where you may edit the existing word or enter a new word. After pressing ENTER, the word is checked against the dictionary.

G   Toggles global replacement on or off. When global replacement is on, all words in the document with the same spelling as the one you corrected are replaced with the corrected word. When global replacement is off, only the current word is replaced.

In addition to the standard dictionary provided with WordStar, specialized dictionaries for the legal, medical, and financial professions are also available from MicroPro.

CHECK INDIVIDUAL WORD ($^\wedge$QN)

To check the spelling of a single word, place the cursor on the word and select $^\wedge$QN. The menu shown previously is displayed. If the word is spelled correctly, the definition will be displayed at the bottom of the window. Also, a list of words with similar spellings will be displayed. Note too that you can press the letter M to see additional words if more are available.

CHECK KEYBOARD ENTRY ($^\wedge$QO)

To check the spelling of a word not already in your file, select $^\wedge$QO. The Spell Check window below is displayed.

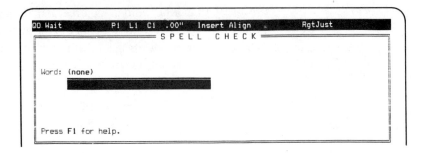

Type in a word and press ENTER; the Spelling Check menu is displayed. Again, if the word is spelled correctly the definition, if available, is shown along with a list of similarly spelled words.

PERSONAL DICTIONARY FROM PREVIOUS RELEASE

In addition to the main dictionary of over 100,000 words, WordStar gives you the ability to create a personal dictionary. A summary of the personal dictionary properties is listed below.

- Words from your file are added to the personal dictionary when A is selected from the Spelling Check menu.

- You may also add words directly to this dictionary by opening the file PERSONAL.DCT in WordStar's nondocument mode and keying in the words. Be sure to key in the words in alphabetical order or else use the sort command, ^KZ, to sort the words in ascending order.

- To use a personal dictionary from an earlier version of WordStar, be sure to sort the list in ascending order.

- Spelling checks are faster if the personal dictionary is small. It is, therefore, better to have three or four small dictionaries than one large one. (You can use WSCHANGE to have WordStar prompt you for the one to use with a particular file.)

- Before you rely on an older personal dictionary for use with WordStar 5, check to see if the words are included in WordStar's new expanded dictionary.

USING THE THESAURUS (^QJ)

To select WordStar's thesaurus, select **^QJ**. The following Thesaurus menu is displayed.

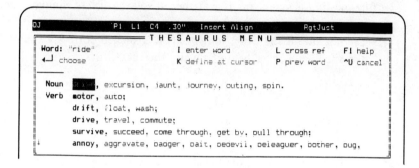

At the top left of the window is the word for which you are seeking a synonym. To the right are the command options and below is a listing of available synonyms. If there are more synonyms than will fit in the window, a down arrow is displayed in the lower left corner (as shown in the preceding illustration). You can scroll the contents of the window a line at a time using the arrow keys or a full page, if enough additional options are available, using the PgDn and PgUp keys.

The commands to the right of the word being checked along with other keys useful with this window are described below.

Command	Function
← →	Moves the cursor through the option list a word at a time in the direction of the arrow.
ENTER	Replaces the word in your document with the word the cursor is on.
ESC	Exits the thesaurus and returns you to your position in the file.
I	Displays the Synonym Lookup window. Here you may enter a selection of your choice. Your entry may be defined and synonyms are displayed.
L	Displays synonyms for the word in reverse video.

P   Redisplays synonyms for the previous word (usually used after L has been selected).

K   Defines the word displayed in reverse video.

At times the thesaurus cannot find the word for which you are requesting a synonym. It will then display a list of similarly spelled words and allow you to select synonyms for any of these words. If you are not sure if the word you specified is spelled correctly you can use the spelling checker before you use the thesaurus.

EXERCISES

1. Spell check the file POLIT1.MD in Example 17B to see the Spell Check windows. This file contains no misspelled words, but it does contain several words for which there is no match in the dictionary.

2. Spell check one of your own files and, where appropriate, add words to the PERSONAL.DCT file. Run the spelling checker again to verify that WordStar no longer stops at any words you have added to your personal dictionary.

3. Experiment with the spelling checker options to become familiar with them.

4. Check the procedures in Appendix C for using WSCHANGE and then code one of the function keys to call a specified personal dictionary.

ADVANCED PAGE PREVIEW

Advanced Page Preview is a new feature of WordStar 5. Page Preview lets you look at or preview the pages of a WordStar file before they are printed. You can see how margins will appear and what the formatting will look like. If different size fonts or italics are used in your file you can see how they will appear in the file before it is printed. Another useful aspect is to preview, on screen, files that are formatted using newspaper-style columns.

To use Page Preview, you will need a graphics adapter installed in your computer. Any one of the more common types — HGA, CGA, EGA, or VGA — work well. All of the screen displays shown in this lesson were produced on a computer equipped with an HGA card and a monochrome monitor. If you are using a different graphics card your screen may show more or fewer pages on multiple page displays.

For a useful trial of Page Preview, a file with several pages is necessary. The sample file used for the illustrations has nine pages. To follow along with this discussion and try the ideas as they are presented, use any one of your multiple-page files. One point to be aware of is that you cannot scroll a page to the left in Page Preview as you can in WordStar. In Page Preview you can only see the text that will print on the standard paper size, 8 1/2 by 11 inches.

SELECTING PAGE PREVIEW (^OP)

To select Page Preview, you can use any one of the following methods while in WordStar's edit mode: (1) press ALT-1; (2) from the Layout menu select Page Preview; (3) press ^**OP**. Before you start Page Preview, keep in mind these points. When you select Page Preview, the first screen display shows the page the cursor was on in the file.

When you open a book the even-numbered page is always on the left and the odd-numbered page on the right. Page Preview is designed to show you how a document will appear when it is printed. If the cursor is on the first page of your file when you invoke Page Preview, then page 1 will appear on the left side of your screen. If you select "Facing page" from the View menu, page 1 will move to the right side of the screen and the left side will be blank. If the initial page is any page but page one, 3 for example, and "Facing page" was selected, page 3 would move to the right half of the screen and page 2 would be displayed to its left.

As always with WordStar, the best way to learn a new feature is to try it. Load into WordStar the multiple page file that you intend to use with Page Preview. Move the cursor to page 2 of the file and press ALT-1. If the file you're loading uses any fonts in addition to the default font, a message will appear briefly on the screen stating: "Building preview font", and then page 2 of your file will appear on the left half of the screen in reverse video. Your display will be similar to the one below.

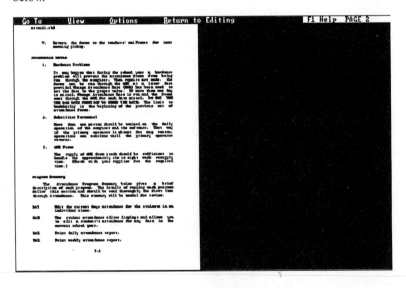

The initial presentation of a page requires only half of the screen. Keep in mind that the purpose here is to examine the format and appearance of the page layout, not to edit or read the file. Obviously, the text quality does not compare to that available while in WordStar's edit mode. Note that the number of the page you are viewing is in the upper-right corner of the screen.

THE VIEW MENU

As is common in WordStar, as well as with its associated programs, there is generally more than one way to accomplish the same thing. Page Preview has its own set of pull-down menus. To make a selection, press the first letter of the menu title. The options to select multiple pages are on the View menu. Press V and the View menu is displayed. A representation of that menu is shown below.

View

```
Entire page
Facing page
Multiple pages
Thumbnail display
2x
4x
Adjust.
```

You can make a selection from the menu by pressing the first letter (or number) of the selection or by using the arrow keys to highlight the desired selection and pressing ENTER.

Selecting View Choices
Using the (+/−) Keys

You can also step through the selections on the View menu by pressing the plus or minus key. This can only be done prior to displaying the menu. Pressing the (−) key moves you through the View options in the order they appear on the menu down to Thumbnail display.

To try this now and see more pages of your file, press the minus key. The screen displays

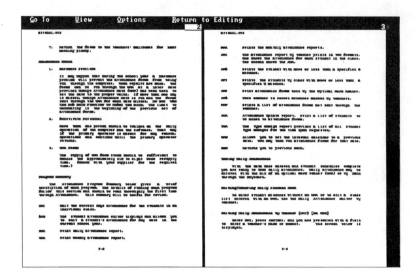

You now have page 2 and its facing page, page 3, on the screen. In this case, note that the page numbers are now in the upper right corner of each page. This occurs when there are two or more pages on the screen. The selected page is the one with the page number in reverse video. Use the left- and right-arrow keys to change the selected page. If two or more rows of pages are displayed, the up and down arrows may be used as well. The selected page is the one that will be displayed when any single-page view is selected.

To view more pages press the minus key again. The screen now displays eight pages. The display starts from the selected page.

Thumbnail Displays

The smallest set of pages your screen can display is referred to as the Thumbnail display. Select Thumbnail display from the View menu or, with the previous display on the screen, press the minus key one more time. A display with 21 pages appears on the screen—depending, of course, on the size of the file you are working with and the type of graphics adapter installed in your computer.

Enlarging the Image Size (2x, 4x)

To reverse this process of seeing more and smaller pages, press the plus key. The page sizes that now appear on the screen appear in the reverse order of the sequence followed when the minus key was pressed. You may also "pull down" the View menu and select your choice directly from that menu.

If you reverse the process with the plus key, when you arrive back at the original screen displayed when you invoked Page Preview and press the plus key one more time, the display enlarges to two times normal size, as shown below.

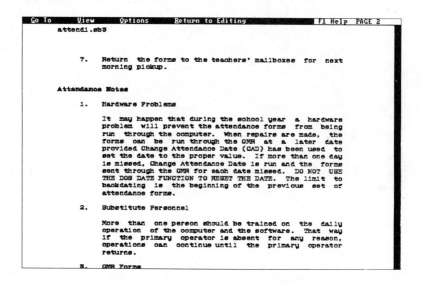

Pressing plus one more time gives you a four-times enlargement.

Adjust View

The final selection on the View menu, Adjust, is available with single-page display and with 2x or 4x enlargements. It lets you move or adjust the screen to view a particular section of a page.

With a single page displayed on the screen, select Adjust. A window is opened in the center of your screen, showing the page you are viewing. A rectangle outlines the upper half of the page. You have six keys to help you position the rectangle over the desired portion of the page. The three keys at the top of the keypad (HOME, Up arrow, PgUp) move the rectangle up and the three keys at the bottom of the keypad (END, Down arrow, PgDn) move the rectangle down. If the Page Preview display is in 4x enlargement the rectangle in the adjust positioning window covers approximately an eighth of the page. You now have eight keys available to position the rectangle. The four arrow keys move the rectangle in the direction of the arrow. The four corner keys on the numeric keypad, HOME, PgUp, END, and PgDn move the rectangle diagonally over the page. When the rectangle is positioned correctly, press ENTER; the positioning window closes, and the portion of the page in the rectangle fills your entire screen. This gives you a very detailed view of that portion of the page.

THE GO TO MENU

Regardless of what page is displayed when you start Page Preview, you can very quickly move to any page in your file by making selections from the Go To menu. Its choices are shown below.

Goto

```
Specified page
First page
Last page
Next page
Previous page
```

Choices from the Go To menu can be selected regardless of what view option is in effect from 4x to Thumbnail. Also, when you make your Go To selection, the view option does not change.

OPTIONS MENU

Additional selections are available from the Options menu, as shown in the following illustration.

Options

```
Automatic scan
Scan range
Grid display On/Off
```

The option, Automatic Scan, moves you quickly through a file, from the first to the last page, giving you a brief look at each page.

Scan Range allows you to select the range of pages to scan. Again you are provided with a brief look at each page. The choices on the Scan Options menu, like those on the Go To menu, can be selected with any view option in effect and that view will be retained during the scanning process.

The last choice on the Options menu is Grid Display On/Off. This option places a grid on the display that allows you to accurately check the placement of any graphics or special formatting you have placed in the file. The grid display is available for full-, 2x-, and 4x-page representation.

RETURN TO EDIT MODE

You can return to WordStar's edit mode in either the page you were viewing while in Page Preview or the page you were in when you invoked Page Preview. From the Return menu, select either Original page or Current page. You can also return to WordStar's edit mode by selecting ALT-1 for Current page or ALT-2 for Original page. Pressing ESC will also return you to WordStar's edit mode in the Original page.

EXERCISES

1. Practice using all of the options on the View menu. Use the $+/-$ keys to change the page size you are displaying.

2. Select at least two different sections of the multiple-page file you've been using with Page Preview and change the font to something other than the default font. Look at those sections of the file in Page Preview using 4x enlargement.

3. Prepare a file with newspaper-style columns. Keep in mind that the total number of inches used for margins, text for each column, and columns between text must be less than the width of the display page. Use Page Preview to check the placement of the file on the page before you print the file.

4. Practice using the Adjust option so that you can quickly get a close-up view of a particular portion of a page.

5. If you use graphic displays in your documents, work with the Grid option to become familiar with formatting a page that contains a chart or some other type of graphic representation.

PROFINDER

 ProFinder is a new feature of WordStar 5. The purpose of ProFinder is to make it easy to organize and work with the files on your hard disk: not just WordStar files but any files. ProFinder performs functions you've probably wished DOS would do and wondered why it didn't. Below are the highlights of ProFinder functions.

- Select groups of files to copy, move, or delete.
- Sort files on a directory by name, extension, time/date, or size.
- Search all files in a subdirectory for specified text or title.
- View the contents of a WordStar or ASCII file.
- Create your own menu.

You can start WordStar from ProFinder. ProFinder can be used with floppy disks, but its primary function, organizing files on a disk, is much more useful to those using a hard disk.

STARTING PROFINDER

Be sure that ProFinder is on a directory that is included in the path so that it may be loaded from any directory on your hard disk. (A discussion on using the path is in Appendix D.)

To run ProFinder, type **PF** and press ENTER. (If you placed PF on a subdirectory other than WS5, the first time you type PF, a screen message will ask where the PF files are located. Enter the subdirectory name in the dialog box provided and press ENTER.) The screen displays the current directory along with some other information as shown in the following illustration.

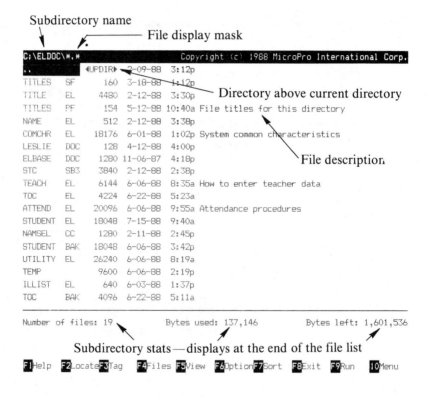

Subdirectory name

File display mask

Directory above current directory

File description

Subdirectory stats—displays at the end of the file list

Along the bottom of the screen is a display showing the option for each function key. Shortly, we'll look at each of these options.

USING PROFINDER

With your experience in WordStar, you will find ProFinder easy to use. They use the same commands to perform the same functions.

Moving Through the File List

After you open ProFinder, the screen displays the files list of the current directory. The cursor is waiting at the UPDIR selection (signified by ..) for your command. As you might expect, you use the standard WordStar commands for moving about the file list. The following table shows both the keypad and WordStar keys to use for each cursor command.

Keypad	WordStar	Function
↑	^E	Scrolls up one file name
↓	^X	Scrolls down one file name
PGUP	^R	Scrolls up one screenful
PGDN	^C	Scrolls down one screenful
HOME	^QE	Moves the highlighting to the top of the screen
END	^QX	Moves the highlighting to the bottom of the screen
^HOME	^QR	Moves the highlighting to the beginning of the list
^END	^QC	Moves the highlighting to the end of the list
	^Z	Scrolls the screen up one file name
	^W	Scrolls the screen down one file name

The following table contains additional key commands for this portion of ProFinder.

Key	Command Description
ENTER	Pressing ENTER with a directory name highlighted displays the file list for that directory. Pressing ENTER with a file name highlighted displays the file just as if you pressed F5 to view the file (discussed shortly).
	Pressing . (period) at any position in the file list displays the directory above "UPDIR", the current directory.
A-Z	Pressing a single letter moves the cursor to the next name in the file list starting with that letter.
SHIFT A-Z	Pressing SHIFT and a letter moves the cursor back to the previous file name starting with that letter.
→	Pressing the right-arrow key moves the cursor to the Title field.
F1-F10	These keys select the function associated with that key. A discussion of each function is presented shortly.
TAB	Pressing TAB moves the cursor from the file list to the Title field.
ESC	In general, pressing ESC moves the cursor to your previous command position. From the file list, ESC exits to DOS in the directory you were in when ProFinder was loaded. (F2 exits to DOS in the current directory.) If the cursor is in a dialog box, ESC returns it to the previous dialog box.
\	Pressing \ presents a dialog box for you to enter a path and allows you to restrict which file names are displayed in the file list. For example, *.DOC displays only files with the extension DOC in the current directory.
*	Pressing the asterisk lists all files on the current directory (and ends the restrictions entered with \).
:	Pressing a colon displays a dialog box showing the current disk drive and allows you to enter the appropriate letter for a new drive.

Title Field

The limitation of eight letters for a file name plus three letters for the extension can be somewhat restrictive in giving a clue about the contents of a file. ProFinder makes available a Title field. This field gives you 39 spaces in which to enter a file description. An example is shown in the first screen illustration in this lesson.

Follow these guidelines for entering titles.

- Move to the Title field by pressing the TAB or the right arrow key.

- The standard WordStar editing features are available for making an entry in the Title field.

- The insert key, INS, is a toggle just as it is while you are in Word-Star. Try it and notice that while in insert mode, the shape of the cursor changes.

- To move from the Title field back to the file name column press ENTER or ESC.

Working With ProFinder's Functions

With many of ProFinder's functions, an Option window or a dialog box is displayed listing a set of choices or requesting information. The following procedures enable you to make selections from the option windows.

- To select an option, press the first letter of its description. You may also use the up- and down-arrows to move the cursor to highlight the option; then press ENTER to accept the highlighted option.

- If the option is a toggle (offers yes or no) press the first letter of the option to highlight it and press ENTER to toggle between yes and no. Use the up- or down-arrow or the first letter of another option to select a new option.

- In some cases selecting an option will open another Option window (there may be several). Selections from these subsequent windows follow the procedures outlined above.

- You can only make a selection from the last Option window opened.

- Selecting an option in the last option window or pressing ESC (in any option window) returns you to the previous window.

Hot Keys (GREY+, GREY−)

The term "hot key" refers to a key that takes immediate action when pressed. There are two hot keys in ProFinder, Flip (the GREY+ key) and Copy (the GREY− key).

Flip flips between WordStar and ProFinder and Copy copies a block of information selected from a file, while in ProFinder, to a file being edited in WordStar.

FLIP   To use the flip hot key, load ProFinder and use its functions to locate the file you want to edit with WordStar. Highlight the file name in the file list and press the GREY+ key. WordStar is loaded along with the selected file. You are in WordStar at the beginning of the selected file and may proceed with the editing. At any time you can switch back to ProFinder by pressing the GREY+.

If you use this method to enter WordStar (pressing the GREY+ key while in PF), the following save/exit rules apply.

- Pressing the GREY+ toggles you back and forth between WordStar and ProFinder.

- If you save a file and exit WordStar you return to PF.

- To exit PF you must already have closed and *exited* WordStar — not just closed the file and returned to the opening screen.

COPY   Use the copy hot key, GREY−, to copy files or blocks of data into the file you are editing with WordStar. While in ProFinder you can block a portion of a file (you will learn how shortly), flip back to WordStar, and by pressing GREY−, transfer the blocked material into your WordStar file. You can also copy a file into the one being edited by highlighting its name in PF, returning to the file being edited, and using ^KR to read in the file.

To open a new file using this method, again, you must close the current file and *exit* WordStar. You will be back in PF where you can highlight a file and press GREY+.

Now let's look at each of ProFinder's functions.

Help (F1)

Pressing F1 presents a help screen. The help screen in turn lists the 10 function keys, F1 through F10. You may then select additional help for any one of these functions by highlighting it and pressing F1. (Pressing ENTER or the function key itself will select the function, not help with the function.) For each function highlighted and selected, other than the immediate commands F8 (Exit) and F9 (Run), the F1 key provides additional help screens. Also, as you move to various sections of a function, further help screens are available—always by pressing F1.

Locate (F2)

Locate allows you to search the files or file titles on a subdirectory for specific text. The search can include three strings, or text groups, with up to 20 characters in each group. Press F2 and the first LOCATE dialog box is displayed.

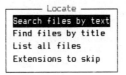

```
────── Locate ──────
Search files by text
Find files by title
List all files
Extensions to skip
```

Select either of the first two options and the window, "Text to locate," is displayed.

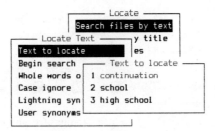

```
────────── Locate ──────────
        Search files by text
── Locate Text ──────y title
Text to locate        es
Begin search   ── Text to locate ──
Whole words o│ 1 continuation
Case ignore   │ 2 school
Lightning syn│ 3 high school
User synonyms
```

In this illustration a string (text) has been entered for each of the three options. You'll see the result shortly. If you are searching for titles you may use any portion or the whole title for your search. After the search text is entered, press ESC to move to the ProFinder Text window.

Here each option is a toggle. Make your choices, select "Begin search", and press ENTER.

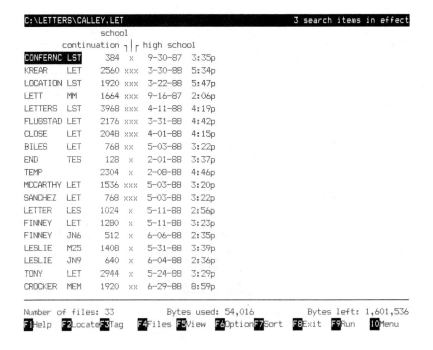

Notice that the three search strings are shown at the top of the illustration. An *x* is printed in the column below each to indicate which files the strings were found in.

EXCLUDING FILES TO SEARCH   Normally in a search you are only interested in looking through files that contain data you entered. The Locate window offers the option "Extensions to skip." With this option you can limit the files that are searched. There is room for 15 extensions in the list. Select this option and you'll see that 13 are provided; you may enter another two. Pressing F3, Clear, with an extension highlighted deletes the entry. Pressing F4, Zap, deletes all entries in the extension list. Any extensions that are cleared may then be replaced with extensions of your choice.

Tag (F3)

To tag or select a file or group of files, highlight the file name by pressing F3. You can now perform one of the file functions displayed when the Files key, F4, is pressed (discussed next). The following illustration shows a sample display with tagged files.

```
C:\LETTERS\*.*
..              ◀UPDIR▶  1-11-88   2:28p
ASCII    WS      1792  3-22-88   5:51p
SL87     88      1152 10-02-87   9:51a
LESLETT  LET      384  4-28-88   2:07p
LESLIE   45       384  4-05-88   3:46p
RETADD   EAS      384  6-01-86  10:54p
LESLIE   LET      512  4-13-88   3:54p
MAILMERG HED      256  9-31-87   2:40p
WISUPDAT INS      512  9-15-87   3:14p
TEMPS           1536  3-28-88   7:46p
CESAREC  MEM     5760  2-29-88   9:09a
LESLIE   MEM      256  4-01-88   2:57p
KAREN    LET      768  3-04-88   5:28p
BERNICE  LET     1920  3-04-88   5:33p
THOMAS   MEM     5760  3-18-88  10:25a
NANCY    NOT     2688  3-09-88   9:31a
LARSEN   LET     2432  3-14-88   4:56p
RICHARD  NOT      256  3-15-88   5:16p
MIZENER  LET      896  3-10-88   6:06p
CONFERNC LST      384  9-30-87   3:35p
KREAR    LET     2560  3-30-88   5:34p
CESARE2  MEM     1664  3-25-88   4:33p
MBHANDBK FRM     2048  3-18-88   6:48p
F1Help  F2Locate F3Tag  F4Files F5View  F6Option F7Sort  F8Exit  F9Run  10Menu
```

If you tag a file in error, return the cursor to the file name and press F3 again. It acts as a toggle, selecting or deselecting the highlighted file each time it is pressed.

Files (F4)

Select F4 and a dialog box is displayed showing the file commands available with ProFinder.

A couple of these commands are familiar from DOS. The rest are only available in ProFinder.

COPY/MOVE FILES   Selecting Copy or Move copies or moves the tagged files to the subdirectory you select and opens a dialog box where you may enter the directory you wish to copy or move the files to. Move has the effect of copying files to a new directory or disk and deleting their names from the original directory in a single operation.

DELETING FILES   Selecting Delete deletes all tagged files. If you have not tagged any files, you can still delete a file by entering its name. You may also indicate a path. When you select delete you are given the opportunity to confirm the selection before deleting begins.

TIME/DATE STAMP   Selecting Time/Date stamp presents a window where you may enter the date and time. Pressing ENTER uses the current date and time (as set in DOS). All tagged files will receive the new date and time. You may also use the DOS wildcards, ? and *, to select groups of files to receive the time/date stamp.

PRINT FILE LIST   Selecting Print File list prints all the file list information for all files on the current directory. It also prints the directory summary at the end of the file list. All tagged files are underlined.

WRITING FILE NAMES   Selecting Writing File Names creates a disk file for the file name. If files are tagged, only tagged files are written to the file. If no files are tagged, all files are written to the file.

SELECTING TAGGED FILES   The option, Selecting Tagged Files, displays only the tagged files on the screen. To change the file list back to the full file list, press the *.

LIST FILES   If a subgroup of the file list is displayed on the screen, you can use the option, List Files, to display the complete list.

FILE TAG BY WILDCARD   Here you can use the standard DOS wildcards, * and ?, to tag groups of files. Any of the file options discussed above may then be performed on that group.

RETAG/UNTAG   Use the Untag option to untag the files in preparation for making a new selection. If you leave the Files option to perform another ProFinder option, when you return to the Files option, you can retag previously tagged files by pressing **R**.

View (F5)

You may view any file that is in WordStar or ASCII format. To view a file, highlight the file's name and press F5.

```
C:\BOOK\EXAMPLE.1                          ◄▦                              ►
      Most  applications  of microprocessing in our  schools  have
 been  on a very small scale and, it seems to me, what we need  at
 the  moment is demonstration of specific benefits that  might  be
 realized  from the purchase and installation  of  microcomputers.
 We currently have thirteen Apple II Plus computers at our  school
 but  our program is an exception to the norm in public  secondary
 education.

      Our  conference,  therefore,  will  focus  on  the  use   of
 microcomputers  in the public secondary school setting  and  will
 incorporate  presentations designed to increase awareness in  our
 administration of the potential benefits of having microcomputers
 in the schools.  I envision  presentations discussing the use  of
 computers in the science curriculum as multidiscipline tools  and
 for administrative applications.
```

```
F1Help  F2Locate F3Prev  F4Next  F5Write  F6Print  F7Begin F8End   F9Open  10Auto B
```

View allows you to quickly display a WordStar or other file. You have a variety of functions that can then be performed. You can

- Move blocks of text to other files
- Write blocks of text to the disk
- View up to three files at a time
- Locate specific text in the file

With a file displayed, press FI to display the Help window. This window shows the WordStar commands that are available to review the displayed file. The display follows.

```
───────────────── Help ─────────────────
You can use these keys while you are viewing the file:

← or ^S  - Previous char      F1 or  ^J - Help
→ or ^D  - Next char          F2 or ^QF - Find text
^← or ^A - Previous word      F3 or ^QV - Find previous
^→ or ^F - Next word          F4 or  ^L - Find next
↑ or ^E  - Previous line      F5 or ^KW - Write block
↓ or ^X  - Next line          F6 or ^KP - Print block
^QS      - Begin of line      F7 or ^KB - Mark begin block
^QD      - End of line        F8 or ^KK - Mark end block
^Home    - Begin of file      F9 or ^OK - Open another file
^End     - End of file        F10       - Auto block
PgUp     - Previous page      ^KH - Hide block
PgDn     - Next page          ^QR - Begin of file
Home     - Begin of screen    ^QC - End of file
End      - End of screen      ^QG - Toggle file format
Space    - Next char
Backspace - Previous char     ^W - Scroll down
Tab or ^I - Tab               ^Z - Scroll up
────────── Press any key to continue ──────────
```

Selecting View (F5) redefines each of the function keys. A more complete description of the redefined function follows.

F1 Help	Display WordStar commands available
F2 Locate	Find specified text
F3 Prev	Preview occurrence of located text
F4 Next	Next occurrence of located text
F5 Write	Write blocked material to disk
F6 Print	Print the file
F7 Begin	Mark beginning of a block
F8 End	Mark end of a block
F9 Open	Open a file (up to three may be opened)
F10 Auto B	Mark the line the cursor is on as a block

VIEWING A SECOND/THIRD FILE   When you press F9 to open a second or third file, ProFinder opens the file whose name the cursor is on. If the cursor is not on a file name, you are prompted to type in a file name. Of course, you may indicate a path for the file.

As each additional file is opened, it is automatically allocated to a portion of the screen. The portion allocated may not be changed. Also, you may only edit or scroll in the last file opened. Pressing ESC closes the last file opened and places the cursor in the previously opened file for editing. Pressing ESC in the first file opened moves the cursor back to the file list.

FILE FORMAT   The default value for format is for WordStar files. If you view another type of file and a lot of strange characters appear, press ^QG to toggle the file format to ASCII. Your option is to select the best of these two formats. The next topic, Options, discusses how to change the default format.

Options (F6)

The function, Options, offers several selections. The following illustration shows the initial window display.

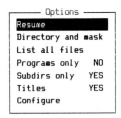

The top option, Resume, returns you to the file list.

The next five options allow you to determine which files and what information are included in the file list. Notice that three of these options are toggles. You can select a file list of only programs, only subdirectories, or you can suppress the display of titles.

CONFIGURE   Selecting the last option, Configure, presents the following option window.

From the configuration window, you can again select several options. Let's look at each.

USER SYNONYM FILE   With this option you can create a synonym file to use with Locate. When you search a file for specific text, it will also search for the synonyms you enter here. For example, you might use Locate to search for "auto". In your synonym file, you could then have car and automobile as synonyms for auto. When entering data for this file all you have to do is place the word you are searching for first and follow it with the list of synonyms, separating the words with commas.

HOT KEY SETTINGS   Selecting "Hot key settings" displays a window where you may change the keys used as hot keys. The default settings are the GREY+ and GREY− keys.

PRINT MARGIN   Selecting print margin displays a dialog box where you may change the left margin used when printing from the View function.

FILE FORMAT   Selecting this option sets the format for the View option (F5). The default format is for WordStar files. The other option available is ASCII, which may be better for viewing files created with other programs. Try each to see what works best with non-WordStar files. Remember, you may also use ^OG to toggle between WordStar and ASCII formats while viewing a file.

TAB SETTINGS   Select "Tab settings" and ProFinder displays a dialog box showing the default tab settings. This option is primarily for those interested in displaying program files. You can set specific tab settings for files with three different extensions. There are two default extensions included, .C and .H (the dots don't display). You can edit the extensions and tabs to whatever you like. The tab set with "Other" will be used for all remaining files.

SAVE SETTING   With this option you can save the changes you made to the default ProFinder settings. When you select this option you are presented with a message at the bottom of the screen display stating "Settings have been saved — Press any key."

Sort (F7)

Sort allows you to sort the files in a subdirectory in a variety of orders. Pressing F7 initially displays the Order and the Sort windows are shown as follows.

The Order window shows the order in which the file list will be sorted if "Begin sort" is selected from the Sort window. Notice that even though the order of the file list is unsorted, the values in the Order window are first by extension and second by name, both in ascending order. This is probably the most commonly requested sort order. If you press ENTER with "Begin sort" highlighted, the file list will be placed in that order. Try it.

To sort the file names in a different order, select "Order of sort" from the Sort window. Press ENTER and a second Order window is displayed. Select one of the four options and again press ENTER. The Direction window is displayed. Select Ascending or Descending (A to Z or Z to A).

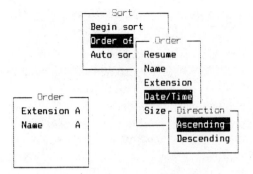

Pressing ENTER will display your selection in the Order window—in this case, "Date/Time A". Press ENTER two more times to select "Resume" in the Order window and "Begin sort" in the Sort window. In a fraction of a second your file names are displayed in ascending order by "Date/time".

Notice in the preceding illustration, the Sort window has the option "Auto sort". This option is a toggle that you can change by pressing ENTER or the letter A. If you select "Yes" for this option, when you change subdirectories, the file names will be sorted according to the display in the Order window.

One further note: If you go to the Configuration window under Options (F6) and select "Save all settings", then any time in the future when you load ProFinder, your directory will be sorted according to the options you saved. Also, you may use the ProFinder install program to change the default values.

Exit (F8)

Select F8 and you immediately exit to DOS in the current directory. (Press ESC to exit to DOS in the directory you were in when you started ProFinder.)

Run (F9)

The Run command allows you to run a program in two ways. (You cannot use this command if you have started WordStar using the hot keys.) The two ways to run a program follow.

1. To run an executable program (one with the extension COM, EXE, or BAT), highlight the program and press F9.

2. Programs with the extension contained in the ProFinder file, EXTLIST.PF, may also be run by highlighting the file name and pressing F9. The extensions supplied in EXTLIST.PF are WKS and DOC. If a file with the extension WKS is highlighted and you press F9, Lotus is loaded and the program is run. If a program has the extension DOC, WordStar is loaded and the file is displayed, ready for editing.

Menu (F10)

The Menu option allows you to design your own menu. Let's start by looking at the sample menu that comes with ProFinder. Press F10 and the following menu is presented.

We'll look at the details in a moment, but first let's get an overall view of how this option can be helpful to a WordStar user. Besides WordStar and the programs that come with it, MailList and TelMerge, you may also use a data base, a spreadsheet, and other programs that are not necessarily associated with WordStar. It makes no difference; you can use the menu you create here to load and run any program. When you are finished with the program selected from the menu, you can automatically return to ProFinder's menu if you wish. Another useful function of the menu is the ability to transfer to a subdirectory and display the file list in a predetermined sort order.

MENU SELECTIONS You select one of the titles displayed in bold in the standard manner by pressing the first letter of the title or using the arrow keys to highlight the title and then pressing ENTER.

Some programs, such as Inset, are designed to stay in memory when you exit them. Having Inset in memory allows you to rapidly move back and forth between Inset and other programs. Sometimes, though, all your memory is required for a particular function. At such times you can remove the Inset program from memory by selecting the "Remove Inset" entry from the menu.

MODIFYING THE SAMPLE MENU Now let's look at the program that produces the menu. The following illustration shows a printout of that file, USERMENU.PF.

```
>Sample Menu
Documents,      /k=":c{enter}{F3}\doc{enter}{F7}{enter}"
<------ Inset -------
Inset,          c:
                cd\inset
                inset
                sf ~d~p
Remove Inset,   c:
                cd\inset
                   ri
                sf ~d~p
<---- PC Outline ----
Normal version,c:
                cd\pco
                pco /r
                sf ~d~p
Small version,  c:
                cd\pco
                pco /r /m=20
                sf ~d~p
<------ Other -------
Lotus,          c:
                cd\lotus
                123
                sf ~d~p
Quit,           /m=quitmenu.sf
```

It looks horrible, doesn't it? Actually, it's not only easy to use, but easy to modify. All you need do is learn how to make a few substitutions to create a menu that is useful to you.

There are two basic entries in the program: (1) the entries that display on the screen, and (2) the commands that tell ProFinder and/or DOS what to do when you make a selection.

MENU DISPLAY   First let's consider the portion of the program that produces the screen display. Notice that everything that displays in the menu has an entry in column 1 of the program. You may also notice the symbols > (greater than) and < (less than) in column 1. Let's see what they do.

The symbol > tells ProFinder that this is the menu title and should be centered. The symbol > must be in column 1.

The symbol < denotes a section of the screen display. It is not displayed in bold and cannot be selected. The symbol < must also be in column 1.

The final display items are the words, such as "Inset," to be selected. These can be directory names, program names, functions, and so on. These selections then require ProFinder or DOS commands or both to be executed. Again, these words must also start in column 1.

Now let's look at the ProFinder and DOS commands in the sample menu program. These commands are carried out when a menu selection is made.

Begin with two ProFinder commands: /k, which is in the second line of the program, and /m, which is in the last line of the program.

The symbol, /k, closes the ProFinder menu and performs the functions that follow. The next illustration demonstrates the effect of /k using the second line of the program as an example.

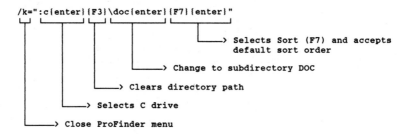

Now let's look at /m. In the last line of the program, /m tells ProFinder to close the current menu and to display the menu shown after the equals sign—in this case, "quitmenu.pf."

To try this command, select Q from the sample menu. You will see the Quit menu on the screen. To view the Quit menu program, open the file with WordStar. Anytime you open a program of this type, be sure to open it in nondocument mode. (If you make a mistake and open the program in document mode, abandon it; don't save it.)

There are two additional ProFinder commands used in the USER-MENU.PF program supplied with WordStar. They are

Symbol	Function
~d	This symbol is replaced with the current drive letter and colon
~p	This symbol is replaced with the current directory path

The purpose of these two commands is to store the current drive and path. In this way, when a menu selection moves off to a subdirectory other than the current one, ProFinder knows how to find its way back to the current directory when the operation you perform is complete.

Now let's look at the DOS commands that are involved in selections to load and to run a program (refer back to the file listing of the Sample Menu). The command sequence is the same for any program. The following is a list of the command sequence using Inset as an example program.

Command	Function
C:	Change to the C drive
CD\Inset	Change to the Inset subdirectory
Inset	Load Inset
PF ~d~p	When finished with Inset return to ProFinder menu

For each of the other menu selections the format is the same; only the directory name and the name of the program are changed.

Now let's go through the process of modifying the menu program to produce a useful menu. The idea, of course, is that you will find the same process helpful in producing a menu useful for *you*.

Besides WordStar, a data base, Q & A; and a spreadsheet, Multiplan are used. The steps to change the Sample menu follow. Also, three subdirectories are entered that can be accessed from the menu. The following illustration shows the USERMENU.PF program after it has been modified.

```
>Walt's Menu
Book,          /k=":c{enter}{F3}\book{enter}{F7}{enter}"
Games,         /k=":c{enter}{F3}\games{enter}{F7}{enter}"
Letters,       /k=":c{enter}{F3}\letters{enter}{F7}{enter}"
<--------- Q & A ----------
Q & A,         c:
               cd\qa
               qa
               pf ^d^p
<-------- WordStar --------
WordStar      ,c:
               cd\ws5
               ws
               pf ^d^p
<------- Multiplan --------
Plan         , c:
               cd\mp
               mp
               pf ^d^p
<------- MailList ---------
MailList      ,c:
               cd\ws5
               wslist
               pf ^d^p
<------- TelMerge ---------
TelMerge     , c:
               cd\ws5
               telmerge
               pf ^d^p
<------ End Session -------
End ,          /m=quitmenu.pf
```

The following steps were taken to change USERMENU.PF to the
preceding illustration. Open USERMENU.PF in WordStar as a nondocument to change the Sample menu.

As you go through these steps, refer to the preceding screen menu.

1. Change Sample to the desired name (in this case Walt's).

2. Insert a blank line and enter the first directories data.

3. To add two more directories, copy the original twice and then edit
   each line to produce the result shown in the preceding illustration.

4. For each program section, substitute new section names, programs, titles, paths, and program names.

5. Change the last section, Quit, to End to keep the first letter of each
   entry unique. If you had both Q & A and Quit on the menu, Q
   would have selected Q & A. It always selects the first entry if
   multiple entries start with the same letter. (This is also the reason
   for using Plan to select Multiplan.)

With the changes complete, pressing F10 displays

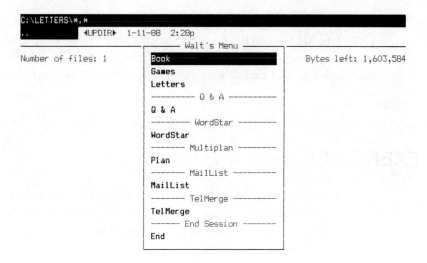

Further comments on menu creation:

- Each selection entry must be separated from ProFinder or DOS commands by a comma.

- ProFinder and DOS commands can begin in any column except column 1. It is common to have them start in the same column as shown here.

- The section titles, including the dashes, should be the same length for a more aesthetically pleasing menu.

DISPLAYING THE MENU FROM A BATCH FILE   People use their computers and programs in a variety of ways. If you find the Menu option works well with your style, you might want to try loading it with a batch file. The details of using a batch file (indicated by the .BAT extension) are discussed in the DOS manual. A simple example is shown here. Open a nondocument file with WordStar, using the name MENU.BAT. In the file, enter **/m=usermenu** as in the following illustration.

```
 C:MENU.BAT      L1      C1         Insert
====File===Edit===Go to===Window===Layout===Style===Other========EDIT===
pf /m=usermenu.pf
```

Place the file in a subdirectory that's in the path. Now, anytime you are in DOS, type **MENU** and ProFinder is loaded and the menu is displayed. If you wish, you could place this command in your AUTOEXEC.BAT file to automatically load and display the menu each time you turn on the computer.

EXERCISES

1. Use MD to create a subdirectory on your hard disk named Exercise. Use the tag option to tag each example from this manual that you entered. Now, using copy in the Files option, copy each example to the Exercise directory.

2. Again using the Files option, delete the files from their original directory. Now, use Move to move the files back to their original directory.

3. Sort the files on the WS5 subdirectory by extension only, in descending alphabetical order.

4. Save the sort order from exercise 3 and exit ProFinder. Return to ProFinder and check that file lists are as you expect. Return the sort order to their default values.

5. If you haven't done so already, modify the sample menu to create a menu that is useful with the programs that you work with.

APPENDIX

NEW AND
MODIFIED COMMANDS

This appendix lists the commands from the traditional menus that are new in WordStar 5, plus those that have been modified from WordStar 4. The numbers indicate the lesson where the command is introduced.

(N)ew or (M)odified	Lesson		Command/Function
N	16	^\	Clear Screen

Opening menu

N	GS	A	Additional
N	GS	S	Speed Write

Quick menu ^Q

N	20	^QJ	Thesaurus
N	6	^Q=	Finds the next font tag in a document
M	12	^QI	When used with + or − moves the cursor forward + or back − a specified number of lines/pages

(N)ew or (M)odified	Lesson	Command/Function	
Onscreen $^\wedge$O			
M	21	$^\wedge$OP	Page preview
M	2	$^\wedge$OE	Prevents a word from being hyphenated
N	8	$^\wedge$OK	Open/switch window (edit 2 pages of one document)
N	8	$^\wedge$OM	Size window
M	2	$^\wedge$OL	Displays page layout settings on screen
N	15	$^\wedge$OZ	Paragraph # ($\rightarrow$, $\leftarrow$, ENTER) To change or select paragraph #

Notes menu $^\wedge$ON (new)			
N	15	E	Creates endnote
N	15	F	Creates footnote
N	15	A	Creates annotation
N	15	C	Creates comment (Non-printing)
N	15	I	Index entry
N	15	D	Edits
N	15	V	Converts to a different type of note
N	15	U	Aligns text in rest of notes
N	15	G	Go to
N	15	L	Spell checks rest of notes

(N)ew or (M)odified	Lesson	Command/Function	
Block menu ^K			
M	8	^KC	Copies block within same window
M	3	^KD	Closes a window and saves notes
M	9	^KR	Copies a worksheet into a file
M	8	^KV	Moves a marked block within same window
M	9	^KW	Adds a marked block to the end of an existing file
N	8	^KA	Window copy
N	8	^KG	Window move
N	16	^KZ	Sorts
N	16	^K?	Byte/word count
M	9	^K.	Sentence case conversion
N	3	^KT	Save as
Print menu ^P			
N	6	^P—	Color
N	6	^P=	Fonts
N	14	^PO	Extended characters
N	6	^P?	Printer driver for this document
M	6	^PY	Selects italic only
N	15	^P.	Enters dots to tab stop (TOC)

(N)ew or (M)odified	Lesson	Command/Function	
Newspaper dot commands			
N	5	.CB	Column break
N	5	.CC x	Conditional column break: x specifies number of lines to be kept together
N	5	.CO	Turns columns on:
		n,g	n specifies number of columns
			g specifies gutter width between columns
N	5	.CO 1	Turns columns off
Dot commands (new)			
N	4	.OC on/off	Centers
N	4	.TB	Tabs
N	15	.P#	Paragraph number format value
N	15	.E#	Endnote initial value
N	15	.F#	Footnote initial value
N	15	.L#	Line number on/off
N	6	.XX	Redefines strikeout character
N	15	.PE	Prints endnotes (section notes)
N	15	.CV f▷e	Converts note type at print time
N	15	.PE	Prints endnote
Changed dot commands			
M	10	.CW	Sets character width in fractional values

(N)ew or (M)odified	Lesson	Command/Function	
M	12	.LQ dis	Leaves print mode up to WS
M	19	.DF	Specifies dBASE files as data files. Specifies Lotus 1-2-3, Symphony, and VP-Planner files as data files
M	19	.FI	Inserts worksheet in a file at print time
M	19	.RV	Selects field names assigned in dBase file as variables for a data file
M	5	.AW	Auto align
M	12	.LQ	Lets WS choose print mode
M	5	.RR n	(0-9) numbered ruler lines (uses preformatted ruler that you set up in WSCHANGE)
M	11	.HE e/o	Even/odd headers
M	11	.FO e/o	Even/odd footers
M	12	.PC 0	Centers page no.

The following dot commands can be set in fractional values. The default is tenths of an inch.

M	10	.LH	
M	10	.CW	
N	4	.TB	
M	10	.PO	
M	10	.PO o/e	Specifies odd or even pages for the page offset

The following dot commands can have relative values in addition to fractional values (such as +5 −5...). For example, you can move the right margin 1.3 inches further to the right with the dot command .RM+1.3″.

(N)ew or (M)odified	Lesson	Command/Function	
M	5	.RM	Right margin
M	5	.LM	Left margin
M	5	.PM	Paragraph indent

Control commands that insert dot commands

M	12	^OJ	Inserts .OJ in the file
M	2	^OL	Inserts .LM in the file
M	2	^OR	Inserts .RM in the file
M	2	^OS	Inserts .LS in the file

Page preview

N	21	ALT-1	Starts advanced page preview
N	21	ALT-2	Quits advanced page preview
N	21	+/−	Used to zoom in and out of page preview

Changes that can be made in WSCHANGE (new)

N	App.C	Save (^KD) automatically every few minutes
N	App.C	Choose shape of cursor
N	App.C	Change cursor speed
N	App.C	Block file size
N	App.C	Convert WS 5 files to earlier releases

APPENDIX

REFERENCE CODES

This appendix lists three types of reference code: flag characters (Table B-1), status line codes (Table B-2), and character codes for both the standard and extended character sets (Table B-3).

Flag	Meaning
<	This line ends with a hard carriage return.
	A blank space in the flag column means the line ends with a soft carriage return produced by word wrap within a paragraph.
P	This is a page break; a new page begins below this line.
F	This line ends with a form feed produced by the $^\wedge$PL command.
C	This is a column break.

TABLE B-1   Flag Characters (Courtesy MicroPro International Corp.)

Flag	Meaning
^	The file ends on or above this line.
+	Text on this line extends beyond the right edge of the screen.
.	The dot command on this line changes the on-screen format and the printout.
:	The dot command on this line changes only the printout.
?	The dot command on this line is not recognized by WordStar.
!	The dot command on this line changes the on-screen format and the printout; it works best if it's placed at the beginning of a page.
-	This line ends with a carriage return but without a line feed (produced by ^P return); it will be overprinted by the next line.
J	The line ends with a line feed but without a carriage return (produced by ^PJ); the next line will print on the line below but may not begin at the left margin.
B	The beginning block marker is in this line.
K	The end block marker is in this line.

TABLE B-1   Flag Characters (Courtesy MicroPro International Corp.) (*continued*)

Information	Meaning
Command	Any command that is in progress.
File name and drive	Name and location of the file you're editing.
Wait	Displayed in place of the file name during lengthy operations and when WordStar is accessing the disk. If you type quickly while this message is displayed, you may lose some of the characters you type.

TABLE B-2   Status Line Information (Courtesy MicroPro International Corp.)

Information	Meaning
Cursor indicator	Shows the page, line, column number, and inches of the cursor's present position.
Insert	Indicates that insert is on. (The INS key or $^\wedge$V turns on and off.)
Prtect	Indicates that the document you're working on is protected.
Align	Indicates that auto-align is on for this text. (.AW switches it on and off.)
RgtJust	Indicates justification is on. ($^\wedge$OJ, .OJ, and Right-justify text on the Layout pull-down menu switch it on and off.)
Mar-Rel	Indicates that margin release is on. ($^\wedge$OX and Margin release on the Layout pull-down menu switch it on and off.)
LinSp-n	If the line spacing is anything except 1 (single spacing), indicates the current line spacing.
Column	Indicates you are in column mode.
ColRepl	Indicates you are in column mode and column replace is on.
Decimal	Displayed when you use TAB or $^\wedge$I to move the cursor to a decimal tab.
Replace? Y/N	Appears during find and replace operations when you need to decide whether to replace the word at the cursor.
Large-File	Displayed when the document you are editing becomes so large that only 3K of working memory are left, or when the document is too large to fit entirely in working memory.
Dot-Limit	Warns you that the number of dot commands in the document is more than the number that WordStar can keep track of during editing. (The document will print correctly.)

TABLE B-2   Status Line Information (Courtesy MicroPro International Corp.) (*continued*)

Information	Meaning
Printing	Appears when you are printing in the background.
Print wait	Appears when you are printing in the background and printing is paused. When you see this message, choose Print a file from the File pull-down or press ^**KP** while editing or **P** at the classic Opening menu. Then choose the appropriate command when you are ready to resume printing.

In nondocument mode, the status line is slightly different. A nondocument status line differs from a document status line as follows:

Cursor indicator	Because nondocuments have no pages, the indicator shows only line and column numbers. The line number can be as high as 65535, and the column number can be as high as 999.
Auto-In	Displayed when auto indent is on. (^6 switches it on and off.)

TABLE B-2   Status Line Information (Courtesy MicroPro International Corp.) (*continued*)

ASCII Value	Character	ASCII Value	Character	ASCII Value	Character
0	Null	12	Form-feed	24	↑
1	☺	13	Carriage return	25	↓
2	☻	14	♫	26	→
3	♥	15	☼	27	←
4	♦	16	►	28	Cursor right
5	♣	17	◄	29	Cursor left
6	♠	18	↕	30	Cursor up
7	Beep	19	‼	31	Cursor down
8	◘	20	¶	32	Space
9	Tab	21	§	33	!
10	Linefeed	22	▬	34	"
11	Cursor home	23	↨	35	#

TABLE B-3   ASCII and Extended Character Set

ASCII Value	Character	ASCII Value	Character	ASCII Value	Character
36	$	74	J	111	o
37	%	75	K	112	p
38	&	76	L	113	q
39	'	77	M	114	r
40	(	78	N	115	s
41	)	79	O	116	t
42	*	80	P	117	u
43	+	81	Q	118	v
44	,	82	R	119	w
45	-	83	S	120	x
46	.	84	T	121	y
47	/	85	U	122	z
48	0	86	V	123	{
49	1	87	W	124	¦
50	2	88	X	125	}
51	3	89	Y	126	~
52	4	90	Z	127	⌂
53	5	91	[	128	Ç
54	6	92	\	129	ü
55	7	93	]	130	é
56	8	94	^	131	â
57	9	95	_	132	ä
58	:	96	'	133	à
59	;	97	a	134	å
60	<	98	b	135	ç
61	=	99	c	136	ê
62	>	100	d	137	ë
63	?	101	e	138	è
64	@	102	f	139	ï
65	A	103	g	140	î
66	B	104	h	141	ì
67	C	105	i	142	Ä
68	D	106	j	143	Å
69	E	.107	k	144	É
70	F	108	l	145	ae
71	G	109	m	146	Æ
72	H	110	n	147	ô
73	I				

TABLE B-3   ASCII and Extended Character Set (*continued*)

ASCII Value	Character	ASCII Value	Character	ASCII Value	Character
148	ö	184	⌐	220	▬
149	ò	185	╣	221	▌
150	û	186	‖	222	▐
151	ù	187	╗	223	▬
152	ÿ	188	╝	224	α
153	Ö	189	╜	225	β
154	Ü	190	╛	226	Γ
155	¢	191	┐	227	π
156	£	192	└	228	Σ
157	¥	193	┴	229	σ
158	Pt	194	┬	230	μ
159	f	195	├	231	τ
160	á	196	—	232	Φ
161	í	197	+	233	θ
162	ó	198	╞	234	Ω
163	ú	199	╟	235	δ
164	ñ	200	╚	236	∞
165	Ñ	201	╔	237	$\varnothing$
166	ª	202	╩	238	$\in$
167	º	203	╦	239	$\cap$
168	¿	204	╠	240	≡
169	⌐	205	=	241	±
170	¬	206	╬	242	≥
171	½	207	╧	243	≤
172	¼	208	╨	244	⌠
173	¡	209	╤	245	⌡
174	«	210	╥	246	÷
175	»	211	╙	247	≈
176	░	212	╘	248	°
177	▒	213	╒	249	•
178	▓	214	╓	250	·
179	│	215	╫	251	$\sqrt{\ }$
180	┤	216	╪	252	^{n}
181	╡	217	┘	253	^{2}
182	╢	218	┌	254	■
183	╖	219	█	255	(blank 'FF')

TABLE B-3   ASCII and Extended Character Set (*continued*)

CUSTOMIZING WORDSTAR

There are two ways to modify WordStar: by using the dot commands or by using the program WSCHANGE discussed here. You use dot commands to change the options for an individual file. The options you modify with WSCHANGE will be in effect for all files loaded by Word-Star. WordStar comes with most options set correctly for the user, but it is the rare user who doesn't want to change at least one of the default settings. Fortunately, WordStar 5 makes modifying the optional settings very easy. These settings can be modified as many times as you like, so feel free to experiment—you can always change the settings again. The changes made with WSCHANGE do not affect your ability to modify an individual file by using dot commands.

MULTIPLE VERSIONS OF WORDSTAR

Besides modifying the copy you work with daily, you may find it worthwhile to create different versions of WordStar. For example, you might have a graphic version where most of the 40 function key commands are implemented to produce graphic symbols. You can create such a version with WSCHANGE, naming the file WSG (for WordStar Graphics), for example. When you want this version, you would load it by typing **WSG**. You would still load the everyday version by typing **WS**. (Remember, though, that WordStar is copyrighted, and you cannot make extra copies of the program or of any special versions you create and distribute them to others.)

LOADING WSCHANGE

Log into the subdirectory WS5, type **WSCHANGE WS**, and press ENTER. This command loads the program WSCHANGE, which in turn loads the WS.EXE file that contains WordStar's operating instructions. The program WS.EXE is the one that is modified during this process. The screen displays the Main Installation menu, shown here.

```
                        Main Installation Menu

    A  Console......Monitor            Function keys        Video attributes
                    Monitor patches    Keyboard patches     Interface patches

    B  Printer......Install a printer  Choose a default printer
                    Change printer name Printer defaults    Printer interface

    C  Computer.....Disk Drives        Operating system     Patches
                    WordStar files     Directory display    Memory usage

    D  WordStar.....Page layout        Editing settings     Help level
                    Spelling checks    Nondocument mode     Indexing
                    Shorthand          Merge print          Miscellaneous

    E  Patching.....General patches    Reset all settings   Auto patcher

    X  Finished with installation


    Enter your menu selection...      ? = Help
```

When you complete your modifications, the program will automatically be saved, with the changes, as WS.EXE. If you wish to create another version of WordStar as described in the previous section, follow this procedure.

1. Load WSCHANGE—do *not* follow it with WS.

2. At the prompt "What file to load?", enter WS.

3. At the prompt "What file to save changes to?", enter your option —WSG, for example.

Again, after you have completed the modifications, the changes will be saved, in this case with the filename—WSG.EXE.

The assumption here is that you have been working with WordStar and are interested in modification, not the initial installation. There are a great many options that you can modify.

PROMPTED CHANGES TO WORDSTAR

You can make two types of changes to WordStar with WSCHANGE: prompted changes and patches.

We will explore only a few options here, but the process is similar for making other prompted or patched changes. With the menus displayed, you can see that a great many changes are possible. Experiment with these options; remember that you always can change back to the original settings.

CHANGING THE FUNCTION KEY COMMANDS

Those of you who work with the traditional menus will most likely want to make at least one change to the Function Key commands. With the

Main Installation menu on the screen, press **A**; the Console menu is displayed. Select **B** for Function keys, and the screen displays the following:

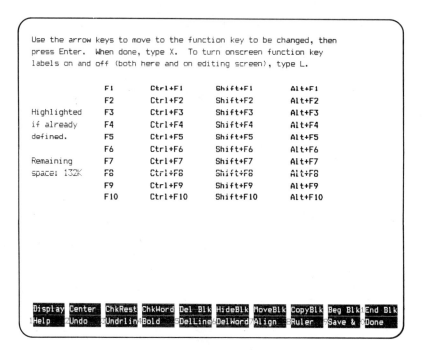

The function keys that are implemented are highlighted. As this screen shows, all the keys are assigned a function. Use the down-arrow key to move the cursor to F7. Let's change this function key command to $^\wedge$B (paragraph reform). The current command is $^\wedge$B$^\wedge$Q$^\wedge$P, which returns the cursor to its starting point after reforming a paragraph. Press ENTER. The following information is displayed.

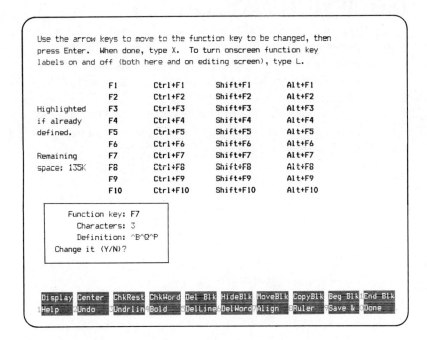

```
Use the arrow keys to move to the function key to be changed, then
press Enter.  When done, type X.  To turn onscreen function key
labels on and off (both here and on editing screen), type L.

                    F1        Ctrl+F1      Shift+F1      Alt+F1
                    F2        Ctrl+F2      Shift+F2      Alt+F2
Highlighted         F3        Ctrl+F3      Shift+F3      Alt+F3
if already          F4        Ctrl+F4      Shift+F4      Alt+F4
defined.            F5        Ctrl+F5      Shift+F5      Alt+F5
                    F6        Ctrl+F6      Shift+F6      Alt+F6
Remaining           F7        Ctrl+F7      Shift+F7      Alt+F7
space: 135K         F8        Ctrl+F8      Shift+F8      Alt+F8
                    F9        Ctrl+F9      Shift+F9      Alt+F9
                    F10       Ctrl+F10     Shift+F10     Alt+F10

        ┌─────────────────────────────────────┐
        │    Function key: F7                  │
        │    Characters: 3                     │
        │    Definition: ^B^Q^P                │
        │  Change it (Y/N)?                    │
        └─────────────────────────────────────┘
```

```
Display Center ChkRest ChkWord Del Blk HideBlk MoveBlk CopyBlk Beg Blk End Blk
1Help  2Undo  3Undrlin4Bold  5DelLine6DelWord7Align  8Ruler  9Save & 0Done
```

Enter **Y** and the question "WordStar keystroke?" is displayed. Press
CTRL-B and then the END key (1 on the keypad). The cursor immediately
moves to the F7 display at the bottom of the screen, and WordStar waits
for you to enter (using a maximum of seven letters) the definition you
would like displayed for the F7 key. Type in your definition and press the
END key.

When you complete that entry, you can also use the arrow keys to
move to any other function key display and change its definition to
something with more meaning to you. You can do this whether or not you
change the implementation of the key.

You also have the option of turning off the highlighted key display
that appears at the bottom of the screen. To turn it off, press **L**. If you turn
off the display here, it will be turned off when you return to WordStar.

When you have completed your modifications, press the END key to
return to the function key table. You can now select another key to modify
or press **X** to retrace your path back to the Main Modification menu. At
that point you can select another section to modify or press **X** if you are
through and wish to return to DOS.

MODIFYING PAGE LAYOUT

Another area where you may wish to make modifications is page layout.
If you commonly use letterhead or a paper size other than 8 1/2 x 11, you
may find it worthwhile to modify your standard copy of WordStar or set
up another version.

To explore this area of WSCHANGE, select **D** from the Main Installation menu. From the WordStar menu select **A**, Page Layout, and the
screen displays the following:

```
                        Page Layout Menu

    A  Page size and margins
    B  Headers and footers
    C  Tabs
    D  Footnotes and endnotes
    E  Stored ruler lines
    F  Paragraph numbering

    X  Finished with this menu




    Enter your menu selection...       ? = Help
```

You have six options. Let's look at A: Page sizing and margins. Select
A. The following screen appears.

```
                    Page Sizing and Margins Menu

     A   Page length.......................11.00"      INIEDT+24 .pl
     B   Top margin........................00.50"      INIEDT+20 .mt
     C   Bottom margin.....................01.33"      INIEDT+22 .mb
     D   Header margin.....................00.33"      INIEDT+31 .hm
     E   Footer margin.....................00.33"      INIEDT+33 .fm
     F   Page offset of even page..........00.80"      INIEDT+36 .poe
     G   Page offset of odd page...........00.80"      INIEDT+38 .poo
     H   Left margin.......................00.00"      RLRINI    .lm
     I   Right margin......................06.50"      RLRINI+2  .rm
     J   Paragraph margin..................(none)      RLRINI+4  . pm

     X   Finished with this menu




     Enter your menu selection...        |  ? = Help
```

You can change any of these default values by selecting the letter in
column 1 and entering a new value in response to the question asked. If
you don't want to change a value, press ENTER. Try changing some of
these values. When you are through with this section, press **X** to return to
the Page Layout menu.

STORED RULER LINES

Let's look at one more option on the Page Layout menu — Stored Ruler
Line. WordStar 5 comes with 10 stored ruler lines.

The first four, .RR0 through .RR3, are preformatted as you saw in
Lesson 5. You can set up the last six, .RR4 through .RR9, to contain
whatever margins and tabs that are convenient for your work. Actually,
you can modify the first four as well.

Selecting option E from the Layout menu allows you to modify any
of the 10 stored ruler lines. Select **E** and the screen displays

```
                        Stored Ruler Lines Menu

 A  Default ruler line
 B  1st stored ruler line
 C  2nd stored ruler line
 D  3rd stored ruler line
 E  4th stored ruler line
 F  5th stored ruler line
 G  6th stored ruler line
 H  7th stored ruler line
 I  8th stored ruler line
 J  9th stored ruler line


 X  Finished with this menu




 Enter your menu selection...        ? = Help
```

Just as with the page sizing screen, you choose a letter from the left-most column to select the stored ruler line you wish to modify. Notice that option A is the default ruler line. If you change the default ruler line, all files that you open will initially have that ruler line.

Select a ruler line to modify and your screen display will be similar to the one below.

```
                          Ruler Line #4 Menu


   A  Left margin..................................00.00"      RLRINI+296
   B  Right margin.................................06.50"      RLRINI+296+2
   C  Paragraph margin............................(none)       RLRINI+296+4  .
   D  Regular tab stops...........................11           RLRINI+296+8
   E  Decimal tab stops...........................0            RLRINI+296+9


   X  Finished with this menu




   Enter your menu selection...       ? = Help
```

Initially WordStar has option E through J the same as the default ruler line. The number of the ruler line you are modifying is shown at the top of the screen. To create a ruler line for your particular requirements, decide on the values you want for each of the items requested on the screen display above. Press the key corresponding to the letter in the left-most column and enter your value in response to the question displayed. You can enter as many regular and decimal tabs as you like.

To see the ruler line you created, open a file and enter the dot command **.RR** # (where # is the number associated with the ruler line you created).

AUTOMATIC FILE BACKUP

For whatever reason, a power failure can occur. If this should happen while you are editing a file, all the work you have put into that edit session is lost unless the file has been saved to the hard disk. With WSCHANGE you set WordStar to automatically save your file whenever the keyboard is inactive for a specified number of seconds that you assign.

To activate this feature follow these steps:

- From the Main Installation menu select **D** for "WordStar".
- At the WordStar menu select **C** for "Other Features".
- From the Other Features menu select **G**, "Miscellaneous".
- Finally, from the Miscellaneous menu select **J**, Auto Backup.

The value you enter in response to "Enter New Value" will be the number of seconds that the keyboard is inactive before a backup automatically occurs. A reasonable value to enter is 10. You can always change it later if you prefer a longer or shorter time period.

RETURN TO DEFAULT SETTINGS

Feel free to experiment as much as you like with the WSCHANGE program. You can quickly change to the original default values with these simple steps.

- From the Main Installation menu select **E** to see the Patching menu.
- Select **C** to return all settings to their original values.
- Confirm your response by entering **Y** to the next question.

D

ESSENTIAL DOS COMMANDS FOR WORDSTAR

DOS offers a wide variety of commands. This appendix discusses only those that are essential to the efficient use of WordStar. For a complete discussion of DOS, consult your PC-DOS or MS-DOS manual.

ORGANIZING YOUR HARD DISK

Your hard disk contains 10 or more megabytes of storage space. That is enough storage for about 3200 pages of typed material. Because a hard disk has so much storage space, it is useful to divide the disk into smaller units.

There are as many ways to organize a hard disk as there are people. What's right is what's convenient and efficient for you. This section points out what you *can* do and offers an example layout. You can modify this layout to suit the combination of programs you use and the way you use them.

A hard disk can be divided into units called *directories.* You may have as many directories as you like. Directories can be further divided into *subdirectories.* The top directory, from which all other directories branch, is called the *root directory.* Below that, at the second level, are the subdirectories that branch from the root. A diagram of one arrangement is shown here.

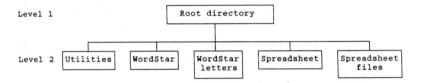

The levels in this diagram could extend downward to include subdirectories off of subdirectories off of subdirectories. The size of any directory or subdirectory is limited only by the memory of the hard disk. So long as space remains on the disk, new material can be added to any directory.

NAMING DIRECTORIES AND SUBDIRECTORIES

Naming directories and subdirectories is the same as naming a DOS file. You may use up to eight letters. You may also use the letter extensions, but that is not common. The root directory is designated by the symbol \. It may not be changed.

Using the previous diagram for dividing a hard disk, let's assign some real names.

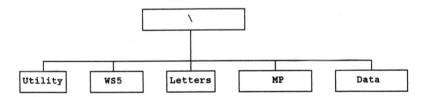

Following is a list of the directories and the contents for this layout.

Directory	Contents
(Root) \	Must contain COMMAND.COM, AUTO-EXEC. BAT, and CONFIG.SYS. It will also contain all directories that branch from the root—in this case, all the directories shown here
Utility	Contains all of the DOS commands not in COMMAND.COM and other utilities you may have purchased
WS5	Contains all of the WordStar operating programs with the extensions .EXE, .OVR, .DCT, and .SYN
Letters	Contains WordStar documents you create
MP	Contains Multiplan operating and data files
Data	Contains Merge Print master documents and data files

The first step in organizing your disk is to decide on the number and names of your directories and subdirectories. Making a diagram like the one shown earlier is a good idea.

MAKING DIRECTORIES AND SUBDIRECTORIES (MKDIR OR MD)

The command for making directories and subdirectories is MKDIR or MD (either name may be used). To make a directory named Letters, you follow the DOS prompt (C>) with

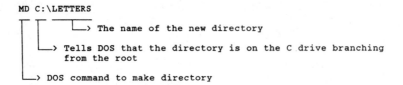

Use the same procedure to create the other directories and subdirectories you have planned.

CHANGING FROM ONE DIRECTORY OR SUBDIRECTORY TO ANOTHER (CHDIR OR CD)

When you have created your directories and subdirectories, you must be able to move comfortably from one directory to another. The command to do this is: CHDIR or CD (Change Directory); again, either may be used. You may move directly from any directory (or subdirectory) at any level to any other directory (or subdirectory). To go from any directory to the root directory, type **CD**. To move from one directory to another on the same level, type **CD** followed by the name of directory you are moving to. For example, to move from the Letters directory to the Multiplan directory, type **CD\MP**. Press ENTER, and you are in the Multiplan directory.

CREATING A PATH FOR DOS TO FOLLOW

When you ask your computer to load and execute a command file, it looks for the file on the directory (or subdirectory) you are logged into. Command files are all those files on your disk with the extension .COM, .BAT, or .EXE. If the command file that DOS is looking for is not on the current directory, the message "Bad command or file name" will be displayed. The solution to this problem is to build a path for DOS to follow that leads to the command file. To build this path, use the DOS command PATH. For the hard disk organization diagram shown here, an appropriate PATH command and path is

PATH=C:\;C:\UTILITY;C:\WS5;C:\MP

Only directories that contain command files should be listed in the path. You may eventually create several directories that contain your WordStar files, but the only directory pertaining to WordStar that needs to be in the path is the one with the WordStar command files (WS5) — not the directories containing the files you create. The same is true for your spreadsheet. The Utility directory must be in the path to access FOR-MAT, BACKUP, or other command files from other directories.

Note the format used by the PATH command. Each directory name is terminated with a semicolon. The drive designation is not essential, but including it is a good habit to get into. With the drive designated, this path will work if you are logged onto the A drive and enter WS to load WordStar. If the drive is not designated, only the logged drive is searched.

USING WILD CARDS (*, ?)

Wild-card characters are very useful with WordStar's Directory command. You can filter out groups of files and display only those groups you are interested in. Two wild cards are available with DOS: the asterisk (*) and the question mark (?). The ? matches any single character of the file name or extension in the position it occupies. For example, the command DIR WS?.ABC displays all files on the directory you are logged onto that have a three-letter name that begins with WS, have any character in the third position, and have the extension ABC.

The * matches a group of characters in either the file name or extension, while *.* matches all file names and extensions. For example, WS*.LET would match all file names starting with WS and ending with the extension .LET; the remaining file name characters, from 0 to 6 characters, could be anything. Entering *.BAK would display all files with the extension BAK. Entering ???85.* would display all files with any characters in the first three positions followed by 85 and any extension.

Consider how these wild-card characters could be used when you assign file names. You can have the directory display only specific groups of files by using the appropriate filters.

TRADEMARKS

dBASE®	Ashton-Tate
DOS™	International Business Machines Corporation
Epson®	Seiko Epson Corporation
Hewlett-Packard LaserJet®	Hewlett-Packard Company
IBM®	International Business Machines Corporation
Lotus 1-2-3®	Lotus Development Corporation
MicroPro®	MicroPro International Corporation
MailList™	MicroPro International Corporation
MS-DOS®	Microsoft Corporation
NEC Pinwriter®	NEC Corporation
ProFinder™	MicroPro International Corporation
Quattro®	Borland International, Inc.
Symphony®	Lotus Development Corporation
TelMerge®	MicroPro International Corporation
VP Planner®	Paperback Software International
WordStar®	MicroPro International Corporation
WordFinder™	Microlytics, Inc.

INDEX

WordStar™ Professional Command Card

CURSOR CONTROLS

Standard keys	Function	Keypad keys
^S	Left character	left-arrow
^D	Right character	right-arrow
^E	Up line	up-arrow
^X	Down line	down-arrow
^A	Left word	^left-arrow
^F	Right word	^right-arrow
^QS	Left end of line	
^QD	Right end of line	
^QE	Top left of screen	HOME
^QX	Bottom right of screen	END
^QG	Forward to specified char.	
^QH	Backward to specified char.	
^QR	Beginning of file	^HOME
^QC	End of file	^END
^QV	To last find operation	
^QI n	Move to page number n	
^QP	Previous position in text	
^QB	Move to block beginning	
^QK	Move to block end	
^K 0-9	Set/hide marker 0 to 9	
^Q 0-9	Move to marker 0 to 9	

Scroll

Standard keys	Function	Keypad keys
^Z	Scroll down line	^PgDn
^R	Scroll up screen	PgDn
^W	Scroll up line	^PgUp
^C	Scroll down screen	PgUp
^Q^W	Scroll up repeat	
^Q^Z	Scroll down repeat	

Delete

Standard keys	Function
BACKSPACE	Del character left
DEL/^G	Del character at cursor
^Y	Del line

Delete, continued

Standard keys	Function
^T	Del right word
^QDEL	Del left side of line from cursor
^QY	Del right side of line from cursor
^QT	Del to designated character
^KY	Del block
^KJ	Del file

Save

Standard keys	Function
^KT	Save as
^KD	Save and exit file
^KS	Save and continue editing
^KX	Save and exit
^KQ	Abandon edit without saving
^PrtScr	Save and Print

Print Functions

Standard keys	Function
^PA	Alternate pitch
^PB	Boldface
^PC	Print pause
^PD	Double strike
^PF	Phantom space
^PG	Phantom rubout
^PH	Overprint
^PI	Column tab
^PK	Indexing
^PL	Insert form feed
^PN	Default pitch
^PO	Binding space
^PS	Underscore
^PT	Superscript
^PV	Subscript
^PX	Strikeover
^PY	Select italic only
^P<ENTER>	Overprint line

WordStar Professional Made Easy

Standard keys — Function

Print, *continued*

Key	Function
^P0 (zero)	Extended characters
^P!	Inline printer control (tag for Inset)
^P*	Graphic
^P–	Color
^P.	Enters dots to tab stop (TOC)
^P=	Fonts
^P?	Printer driver for this document
^P@	Print at specified position

Margins/Tabs/Ruler line

Key	Function
^OL	Set left margin
^OR	Set right margin
^OC	Center text
^OV	Vertical centering
^OX	Release margin
^OI	Tab set
^OG	Temporary indent
^OO	Embedding ruler line

Block Commands

Key	Function
^KB	Mark block beginning
^KK	Mark block end
^KV	Move block
^KC	Copy block
^KW	Write block
^KR	Insert file
^KH	Hide/display block marks
^K'	Change to upper case
^K"	Change to lower case
^KI	Column replace
^KM	Block addition
^KY	Delete block
^KZ	Sort
^K?	Block word/character count
^K.	Sentence case conversion

Standard keys — Function

Find

Key	Function
^QF	Find string
^QA	Find and replace
^Q=	Find next font tag
^L	Find/replace again

Window Commands

Key	Function
^OK	Open/switch window
^OM	Size window
^KA	Window copy
^KG	Window move

Special Functions

Key	Function
^B	Reform paragraph
^U	Undo/interrupt
^J	Help menu
^6	Hard return to soft
^KF	Return to DOS
^OE	Soft hyphen
^ON	Notes menu
^OZ	Paragraph numbering
^QU	Reform entire document
^QQ	Repeat next command
^Q?	Character count to cursor
ESC	Interrupt

Toggles (default screen shown)

Key	Function
^V/INS	Insert on
^OW	Word wrap off
^OT	Ruler line off
^OJ	Justification off
^OH	Auto-hyphen on
^OD	Print display off
^OA	Auto align off
^OB	Soft space dots on
^KN	Block column on
^KL	Directory off

Standard keys — Function

Predefined merge print codes

Standard keys	Function
&#&	Current page number
&_&	Current line number
&@&	Current date
&!&	Current time

Format Codes

	Function
.SV	Sets format codes
(text)	
L, R, C	Left, Right, Center
(numeric)	
9, Z, *, $, –, ., ,, (,).	

Calculator Mode

^QM	Calculator

Shorthand Commands

ESC =	Last result of Calculator
ESC #	Last equation of Calculator
ESC $	Last result in dollar format
ESC @	Today's date
ESC !	Correct time
ESC n	Define own macro
ESC ?	Display/change definition

Spelling/Thesaurus

^QL	Check for rest of document
^QN	Check word at cursor
^QO	Check keyboard entry
^QJ	Thesaurus

Control Commands That Insert Dot Commands

^OI	Inserts .TB
^OJ	Inserts .OJ
^OL	Inserts .LM
^OR	Inserts .RM
^OS	Inserts .LS

Standard keys — Function

Page Preview

Standard keys	Function
^OP / ALT-1	Start advanced page preview
ALT-1	Return to starting page
ALT-2	Return to current page

DOT COMMANDS

Newspaper

Command	Function
.CB	Column break
.CC n	Conditional column break
.CO n,g	Turn columns on
.CO 1	Turn columns off

Page Layout

Command	Function
.LH	Line height
.CW	Character width
.PL	Paper length
.PO	Page offset
.MT	Margin top
.HM	Heading margin
.H1/HE	Heading
.H2	Heading (2nd line)
.H3	Heading (3rd line)
.MB	Margin bottom
.FM	Footing margin
.F1/FO	Footing
.F2	Footing (2nd line)
.F3	Footing (3rd line)
.OC	Center
.P#	Paragraph number format value
.E#	Endnote initial value
.F#	Footnote initial value
.L#	Line number on/off

Page Numbering

Command	Function
.PC	Page number column
.PA	New page

WordStar Professional Made Easy